More Praise for

"Amid the doomsaying and arguing being broadcast through many channels, Isha Judd's message of hope and transformation is refreshing, encouraging, and eminently practical. If you're one of the many people who sense the need for transformation and are looking for clear instruction on how to achieve it, you'll find Isha's words comforting and inspiring."

— Martha Beck, columnist for *O, The Oprah Magazine* and author of *Finding Your Way in a Wild New World*

"Isha has written a glorious book full of important and powerful tools. She is a true slayer of big fat lies and illusions, and I am so excited for every reader of her book to dive in and receive its wisdom."

— Amy Ahlers, author of *Big Fat Lies Women Tell Themselves*

Praise for *Why Walk When You Can Fly?*

"Isha is making an important contribution through her work, bringing consciousness into many diverse communities."

— Shakti Gawain, author of *Creative Visualization*

"The facets explained in this book vibrate on an enlightened level of being and provide a practical way to apply the findings of my research: that the nature of our thoughts profoundly affects our experience of life. In *Why Walk When You Can Fly?* you will learn a simple system to go inward and begin to transform your perception from one based in fear to one based in love and unity in the present moment."

— Masaru Emoto, author of *The Hidden Messages in Water*

"Shows us how to make the most important choice in our lives: to experience the love that is present in every moment."

— Marci Shimoff, *New York Times* bestselling author of *Happy for No Reason*

"There are rare occasions when someone sings the essence of life itself. Isha does this most beautifully and lyrically."

— C. Norman Shealy, MD, PhD, coauthor of
The Creation of Health

"This is an important, even essential book. We live in a time when millions are being called to spread their wings and fly, bringing into manifestation a world that reflects our highest dreams. The only barrier is fear, and Isha gives practical ways to release fear's hold over our lives."

— James F. Twyman, author of *The Moses Code*

"Provides the perfect solution for individuals or couples seeking transcendence and hoping to improve their interactions with others."

— *New Age Retailer*

"Isha teaches with warmth and creativity, sharing stories and anecdotes that help us know that we too can take this journey to our deep heart. Through her practices and suggestions, Isha gives us courage to live fully in this circle of love that is our lasting connection with our true selves."

— Meredith L. Young-Sowers, DDiv, author of
Spirit Heals and *Agartha*

LOVE HAS WINGS

LOVE HAS WINGS

*Free Yourself from Limiting Beliefs
and Fall in Love with Life*

ISHA JUDD

New World Library
Novato, California

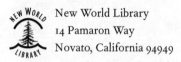

New World Library
14 Pamaron Way
Novato, California 94949

Text design by Tona Pearce Myers

Library of Congress Cataloging-in-Publication Data
Isha, date.
 Love has wings : free yourself from limiting beliefs and fall in love with life / Isha Judd.
    p.   cm.
ISBN 978-1-60868-121-1 (pbk. : alk. paper)
1. Self-realization. 2. Conduct of life. 3. Fear. 4. Love. 5. Spiritual life.
I. Title.
BF637.S4I83 2012
158—dc23   2011045867

First printing, April 2012
ISBN 978-1-60868-121-1
Printed in the USA on 100% postconsumer-waste recycled paper

New World Library is proud to be a Gold Certified Environmentally Responsible Publisher. Publisher certification awarded by Green Press Initiative. www.greenpressinitiative.org

10 9 8 7 6 5 4 3 2 1

CONTENTS

ACKNOWLEDGMENTS

*F*irst I would like to thank Arthur and Annie for taking my discourses and helping me transform them into literature, and my wonderful teachers and students who eternally inspire me and humanity through their commitment to personal evolution.

For supporting my work, I thank Care2.com and *The Huffington Post*, as well as a multitude of publications throughout Latin America, where some of these discourses have already been published. I am, of course, grateful to Marc Allen and New World Library for their continued support, and Kristen Cashman for her careful polishing of this text.

Last but not least, infinite love and thanks to Her Majesty Elizabeth III (her informal title is Betchie the Bulldog) for her constant inspiration and joyful presence.

INTRODUCTION

Laying the Foundation for Love-Consciousness

*I*n the face of economic insecurity and global change, structures are falling, leaving us feeling vulnerable and uncertain. We feel small and helpless before uncontrollable events:
victim-consciousness abounds. Yet what if we really can make
a difference by simply changing our perspective? What if we
can shift to a lighter, more playful perception of life? I believe
that the current state of unrest represents an opportunity for
humanity to reach a new level of consciousness, which I call
love-consciousness, and this book will give you the tools to realize that state of permanent peace and serenity in your own life.

I'm here to share with you how I came to realize that
things really aren't that bad at all, that actually they are rather
more fantastically wonderful than we have ever dreamed of.
It's time to stop worrying and start creating a world worth living in, and it's going to start with you. Yes, you! Don't think

the state of the world is someone else's concern: it's yours and yours alone. Because believe it or not, you're the one who is creating it.

In every moment, you have a choice. You can choose fear, or you can choose love. You can surrender to what is, or you can thrash against it. This book is about empowering you to choose love and joyfully surrender.

MIND MAKEOVER

Modern pop culture is obsessed with makeovers. We are told to change our homes, wardrobes, faces, and thighs as often as we change our clothes. Considering this, it is amazing how resistant we are to internal change. It's time for a mind makeover! Inside our minds, we have a heaving jumble of worn-out old junk: subconscious ideas and opinions that have been out of fashion for longer than knickerbockers and bonnets. It's as if our minds are lost in the run-down comfort of a chintzy old sofa. It is frayed and covered in dust and stains, with the occasional flea, stale crumbs, and the odd bit of chewing gum stuck in its crevices, but it is familiar. Although it is falling apart and in desperate need of replacement, we have become accustomed to it. We have been sitting in it for so long that we don't even notice its strange odor.

Don't you think it's time to redecorate? What if we throw this old couch out on the junk heap and start fresh? The familiar may be comfortable, but if you become stuck in what you know, you will never realize your full potential. Inertia never brings joy: it ultimately leads to dissatisfaction. What if life could become light again, joyful, innocent, celebrating the happiness present in each moment? What if life could go from drama and tragedy to excitement and adventure — from an angst-ridden film noir to a lighthearted romantic comedy, in which you finally discover that your one true love was you, all along?

Who you will become in the future will be defined by who you're being now. How you respond to everything that happens to you each day defines your evolution, and evolution is joy. Ask yourself: *Am I loving myself? Am I becoming the person my heart yearns to be? Am I becoming more love?* As long as you are waiting for something, be it a miracle or a disaster, you are rejecting the opportunity to make new choices right now, to actively generate transformation in yourself and in the world.

So as you start this exciting and exhilarating journey with me, dear reader, this great quest into the very depths of your being, there is one thing I will ask of you. Instead of waiting to see future results, define who you will be in this moment. This is the difference between being a victim and being a creator. A creator determines who she will become, while a victim waits to see what transpires. Every moment you waste thinking about the future is energy that you could use to transform your reality now.

EMPTY IS THE NEW FULL

A Japanese Zen master once received a university professor who came to inquire about Zen.

The master served tea. The Japanese tea ceremony is long and complex, and the scientist became increasingly impatient as the master went calmly through the fifty-four steps of the ceremony. When the tea was ready, he began to fill his visitor's cup. When the cup was full, he continued to pour.

The tea began to overflow, and the professor could restrain himself no longer. "It's already full. No more will go in!"

"Like this cup," the master said, "you are full of your own opinions and ideas. How can I teach you if you have not first emptied your cup?"

In the modern world, we have been taught that by accumulating things — ideas, possessions, knowledge, experience — we will find completion, but in reality, true, vibrant living comes from being empty.

By cramming as much as possible into our every waking moment, filling our senses with an endless barrage of stimulation and distraction, we bury the greatest treasure in existence: our self. Deep down, beneath all the ideas, preferences, opinions, fears, and memories, is your true, eternal being — that which I call love-consciousness. It has always been there and always will be. It is *who we are* at the most fundamental level, yet we have lost sight of it, hidden it from view behind the "stuff" we prize so much. Only by emptying ourselves can we rediscover this most precious of treasures. Emptiness is full of what we deeply want and need.

We cling to the structures that are familiar to us because we think they define who we are. Even if they make us miserable, the alternative seems much less desirable: our fear of change is ultimately the fear of losing our identity — without our belief systems, political affiliations, preferences, and, indeed, our very personalities, who would we be? These ideas about the world and our place in it give us a sense of control; we know where we stand, and we know how to position ourselves in relation to everything and everyone else. But has this illusion of control brought us happiness so far? For the overwhelming majority of us in the modern Western world, the answer is no.

And so, if we wish to find a new vision for life, we must be willing to let go of our old opinions and ideas. Rather than clinging to them — remaining rigid, stagnant, resistant to change — we must be open to receive. We must be willing to evolve. Evolution is the nature of love-consciousness. And what drives evolution? Change. Without change, there is no growth, no life. Rigidity — the lack of or resistance to change — is death. Life must adapt to survive: if we wish to move forward we must be willing to transform, to leave the old behind.

Throughout history, greatness has come from shaking out old opinions. Jesus broke with tradition, as did Buddha. As we evolve, opinions and judgments that we once accepted unquestioningly come to feel antiquated and irrelevant. It's time to empty ourselves of that which we cling to: to relinquish the ideas and opinions that have filled our awareness.

Consciousness evolves. Without change, there is no evolution.

How freeing it is to be empty. To not have opinions, ideas, boundaries, resistance. To say yes to the universe, to say yes to all of creation from a place of joy. It comes from embracing life without interfering, from sweet surrender to *what is*, from falling in love with our present reality. This is the true love affair — the love of an individual for life itself, for oneself, for the joy of being.

So, in this book, more than learning something new, we are going to *unlearn*. In part 1, I will expose some of the most universally accepted illusions, the most fear-based and limiting lies that we have come to accept as our common reality. Several of these illusions stem from a common root, and so there is some overlap among them. However, you may find that you relate to one more than the others or that one seems more salient in your life than the others, so I'm including their different iterations to help you recognize them in the many ways that they manifest themselves.

The rest of the book will address some of the real-life problems that these illusions create in our lives. Part 2 looks at how these illusions crop up in our interpersonal relationships and the various roles we each play in our lives. Rather than perpetuating the stereotypes that have been handed to us and that dictate how we perform our roles as mother, father, man, woman, lover, spouse, worker, or boss, we can come to these roles from a place of love-consciousness and perform them more effectively, joyfully, and compassionately than ever before. Part 3 offers concrete suggestions for embodying love-consciousness in the fast-paced, volatile new century we're living in.

BEACONS TO LIGHT YOUR WAY

Before we get started, we can prepare ourselves by cultivating certain mind-sets and releasing others that hinder us. The guidelines that follow will set the foundation for your life in love-consciousness. Whenever you find yourself confused or full of doubts, you can return to these guidelines to reground yourself in receptivity. Also, many of these guidelines will come up again through the course of the book, and this is a good thing — repetition breeds integration.

Focus on Joy

The first thing we need to do is start focusing on joy — on the beauty, innocence, praise, love, and gratitude inherent in every moment. Isn't it time we did a bit more of that?

How does joy look? This is the wonderful thing about joy: it has no fixed format. Its form is an empty vibration. Joy is like a mountain spring: its effervescence bubbles, teeming eternally from the depths. Its constant spontaneity nurtures and refreshes, flows and replenishes.

Joy doesn't look for what is wrong. It doesn't criticize the external, seeking a culprit for its trials and predicaments. If it did, its waters would soon become stagnant, discolored, and lifeless. Joy is open to love and to being that love. It doesn't have a preconceived idea of how love should be and to whom it should give it.

Rather than waiting for external fulfillment — for pleasure, the next best thing to consume, or a new game to play — instead become that joy. Then move out into the world to share it with humanity.

Stay Present

Joy lives in the present moment, so stop wandering off into the past and future — they've had quite enough of your time already, thank you. It's time to give the here and now — the present, where life is really happening — a bit of sorely needed attention.

Reclaim the Innocence of Childhood

Children have the upper hand over us adults in the happiness department — they approach everything as if it were the first time, completely unfettered by what has come before. They see magic and wonder everywhere they look. Can you imagine how much of a relief it would be to return to that state?

When I was a child, I just was. I wasn't observing myself or measuring the reactions of those around me; I wasn't trying to manipulate, seduce, or control in any way; just to be myself was enough. I had no concept of what it was to be ridiculous, or to be serious: if I was happy, I laughed; if I was sad, I cried. The bottom line: I didn't question my actions. I just was. I was the beingness, being. Carrying the accumulated baggage of adulthood, with its opinions, fears, and misguided perceptions, we have lost this spontaneity.

As you go about your daily life, continually shake the Etch A Sketch of your mind and see things as a child would — without expectations or recriminations. Try to see each person afresh. When the homeless person comes to ask for a coin, give him a smile instead of your usual rebuttal — maybe that was all he ever really wanted. When your tedious mother-in-law calls on the phone, don't answer anticipating her reprimands and complaints. When your boss calls you into her office, don't automatically expect her to chastise you — maybe she'll give you a raise! We are always on guard, expecting that something is wrong. Instead, adopt the emptiness and spontaneous inno-cence of a child; open yourself up to receive with joy.

Lighten Up and Be Playful

One of the saddest things about modern society is that we all take things far too seriously. We feel impelled to conform to that which we "should" be, that which we think the world expects from us. We think, *Don't be ridiculous. Don't speak without being asked. Don't be immature. Don't say what's really on your mind — what will they think?* Self-control and self-criticism have become our way of life, and they drain us of our playfulness and capacity for free self-expression.

We must relearn how to flow from our hearts — to let ourselves look silly, to dance freely, to stop and remind our-selves that life is about laughter and lighthearted joy. Try it. You just might like it.

Let Go of the Need to Be Right

When we become attached to our point of view, it can become more important to us than anything else. As a result, we feel an urgent need to be right, which often requires proving the other wrong, thereby generating conflict. Whenever we feel this need to prove a point, we lose touch with the joy of this moment.

It is easy to tell when an idea or opinion is based in fear: it is accompanied by the need to defend it, to protect the idea from those who disagree. This is the root of fanaticism. Love, on the other hand, needs no defense. It is a crisp, fresh opening to embrace other people's opinions.

When you let go of your need to be right, you learn to flow with the world. In order to do this, you don't have to decide that you were wrong. You simply have to be open to the *possibility* that your perspective may not be the absolute truth, that in the grand scheme of things, it doesn't even matter; that in reality this cherished opinion of yours is just another thought, just another construct of the mind. Simply yielding to that flexibility brings you to a place of greater receptivity.

I don't know is one of the most powerful expressions on the journey of inner growth. When you realize that you don't know something, you open to receive.

Observe yourself. Where have your opinions become more important than peace, than harmony? Ask yourself, *Am I fighting for my ideas, or am I open to seeing a new perspective, to evolving beyond my current understanding?* I am suggesting not that we abandon our ideals but that we keep sight of what is truly important: to always come from a place of love.

Listen to the Voice of Your Heart

The human intellect has many benefits: it has birthed myriad discoveries, conveniences, and inventions that continue to innovate the world we live in. Yet for all its marvelous complexity, it is bound by the constraints of duality. Positive and negative, predator and prey, drought and flood — these opposites form the tenets that the intellect is ruled by. If we wish to experience emptiness, we must go beyond the realm of the intellect. We must get out of the known, and into the void.

The walls the mind has built hold us in limitation. We have become so accustomed to them that they make us feel safe, but these walls also keep us imprisoned in dissatisfaction. Our natural curiosity will always pull naggingly from the subconscious, encouraging us to move beyond the familiar and seek something more. Let us yield to that pull, that innate desire for exploration and discovery, and venture into a new experience of being, beyond everything we have known until now.

There is a knowing that is beyond the mind. Unlike intellectual understanding, which always sees two sides of an argument, this voice never doubts. It trusts itself implicitly and speaks with absolute clarity. When it comes, it will come without warning; suddenly you will find yourself speaking without even understanding why. Yet you will hear the truth in your words. You will feel it. Listen. It's there, lying within. You'll hear it. It speaks from omniscience, with the energy of unconditional love.

Don't Analyze

When you watch a movie, do you wonder how the image got onto your television screen — which satellite it is bouncing off, how the millions of individual pixels combine to create all the different colors? No — that would make the movie really boring! Then why is it we cannot watch life in the same way, innocently embracing the wonderment and mystery, the unexpected chapter waiting around the corner? Why are we always analyzing and dissecting? Analysis mires us in density and complexity, whereas love-consciousness is quite the opposite: it is simple, light, joyful. It opens us up to change, while analysis creates greater rigidity and inertia.

Try just witnessing your life instead of obsessing over the *whys*. What if there is no why? What if it just is, and all you have to *do* is simply *be*? If you try too hard to understand, you will only end up more confused! Instead, try being lighter, more innocent. You will start to understand things from a deeper space, beyond the doubts and uncertainties that inevitably accompany the reasoning of the intellect.

Take Up a Spiritual Practice

Throughout time, people have used spiritual practices to help them transcend suffering and discover inner peace. The important thing is that you go inward, and using a spiritual practice makes it much easier to do so. Devoting time to such a practice on a daily basis yields an ever-deepening self-knowledge and self-sufficiency.

Prayer, meditation, chanting, yoga asana, sense withdrawal, tai chi, journaling — spiritual practice can take an infinite number of forms. I recommend the Isha System, for it is what I used on my personal journey. The facets of the Isha System are an excellent tool for taking you beyond the surface level of the mind. The Isha System and its facets are presented in their entirety in my book *Why Walk When You Can Fly?* For a brief introduction to the facets, turn to Appendix 1 (page 205) of this book. If you practice the facets as you read this book, you'll absorb its teachings much more efficiently.

Embrace the Journey

Imagine you are at the feet of Aconcagua, the tallest mountain in the Andes. *Aconcagua* means "sentinel of stone" in the native Quechua language, and the mountain stands as a beautiful example of conquering the fears of the mind. To rise to the peak of the mountain, you must rise above your fears and focus on appreciation and joy. Then you will be able to witness the world from a transcendent vantage point, in exuberant celebration of the beauty laid out before you.

Yet in order to reach the pinnacle, you must take the journey one step at a time. If you're obsessed with getting to the summit, you won't notice the flowers at your feet. Either you can skip through the daisies and herds of goats grazing on the mountainside (think Julie Andrews in *The Sound of Music*), or you can trudge along solemnly toward your future goal without noticing the beauty all around you. Yet each step is the journey: the love, the joy, the abundance that we're experiencing here, now.

As you journey through this book — and through the rest of your life — focus on the joy around you, all the time, and you will find that you have already reached your destination.

PART ONE

Destroying Our Illusions

N ow that we have adopted the right attitude, one of openness and receptivity, we are ready to begin destroying the illusions that keep us from awakening.

Destruction. It sounds like something negative, but the truth is, wisdom comes from destruction. Emptiness comes from destroying all the chatter — the ideas, opinions, judgments, and concepts that fight for the forefront of our attention. This white noise, this static buzz is what keeps us distracted, blinded, unaware of our true nature, of the glory and beauty of the self. Sitting in self is where the wonderment comes. Being — without anything else, just pure being — is where satisfaction arises. In that emptiness we discover the elusive and achieve all that we have been striving for in the effort to make it, to be somebody, to rise above. It has been there all along, waiting for us to throw up our hands in exasperation and finally stop all the fighting, controlling, taking, and complaining — to finally stop seeking completion outside ourselves.

When we find that inner state, the joy of love-consciousness begins to pervade our every moment, our every action. We become artists, creators, giving our own unique expression to the world. We are not trying to take; we are not focused on how we can benefit. We are giving, adding our own flavor to the mix. Within that sharing of self we begin to find joy and fulfillment.

In this section, by destroying the illusions that cloud our view of ourselves and the world, we will learn to transform victimhood into creativity, uncover the limitations of comfort, destroy the false notion of lack, conquer passivity, transcend discrimination, see through apparent separation, move beyond self-judgment, understand the stifling nature of control, and begin to free ourselves of our own repression.

CHAPTER ONE

Illusion #1: I Am a Victim

EXPRESSED IN THE BELIEF: *Things happen to me that make me less than satisfied.*
REALITY: *I am an infinitely powerful creator.*

The circumstances that have shaped each of our lives are as unique and individual as our personalities — no two people's are the same. Yet our ability to grow as individuals, to evolve into more compassionate, loving, and conscious people, depends not on what has happened to us but on our attitude toward these situations. When faced with hardship, do we lie down or step up? Do we resist, or embrace the situation for growth?

Ultimately there are two attitudes we can take in life: the attitude of a victim and that of a creator.

The victim cannot see beauty, abundance, or the inherent perfection of each moment because he has an idea of how things should be, an idea that has inevitably been violated, an idea that is at odds with what is. This sense of dissonance breeds anger — anger toward life, toward god — but it manifests in the victim as a passive, depressive heaviness, inertia, and seeming disinterest, appearing more like sadness than anger. Ultimately, it represents hatred of self, violence toward self. It is the ultimate rejection of what is: violence toward life.

The only way to break this pattern of victimization is by taking the role of the creator. Creators praise their creations; victims criticize. Creators live in appreciation; victims, in complaint, not taking responsibility. These are total opposites. Creators embrace whatever comes their way. They respond to everything with a *yes*, which enables them to live life in abundance. Victims, on the other hand, are resentful and negative. They cannot see life's inherent perfection or beauty, because they have a rigid idea of how things should look. Shrouded in a cloak of seething passivity, this is the ultimate rage: it is the rejection of existence, the denial of *what is*.

I am responsible.

Whenever I look at my life with a no, with a different idea of how things should be, I am rejecting life. Because I cannot control the game, I will not play. I cannot understand, so I will not accept. Such is the obsessive extremism of a fearful intellect; its complications suck all the joy out of life. Consciousness lives in the union of the heart. When you live from the heart, there are no questions. When you are the absolute, the desperate need to understand disappears; it is engulfed by the pregnant joy of pure being. The heart wants for nothing more when it has found love.

How do I transform myself from a victim into a creator? By focusing on love-consciousness, on the silent depths that lie within us all, until I become the mind without thought. Why?

There is no why. It just is. When you notice yourself resisting what is — thinking, *something could be better in this moment or something is unjust* — let go. Remember that when you flow, when you surrender, you are being god. When you are fighting, you're being a resentful child who won't take responsibility. Nothing could ever be better in this moment, nothing is unjust, because god is everything; you are god within everything; god is joy; and it's all your creation.

Freeing Yourself from Victimhood

Please understand I am not suggesting you intellectually convince yourself that you are not a victim. On the contrary, if you feel like a victim in any aspect of your life, allow yourself to feel it. Embrace your inner victim. Love your inner victim. You will not become free of it by rejecting or judging it. Feel the emotions your feeling of victimhood provokes: sadness, anger, resentment. Scream into a pillow. Cry. Beat on a mattress. Do whatever comes naturally. Embrace your inner victim, and you will soon learn to see through it. As you release these accumulated emotions, the attitude of the victim will lose its charge and soon disappear.

Releasing the Blame

Ultimately, being a creator means taking responsibility for your life. The victim sees responsibility as an uncomfortable concept, a chore: *it is much easier to blame someone else for my discontent.* Yet in reality it is not easier: it simply takes the decision to stop suffering out of your hands. Until you take responsibility for your own happiness, you are a slave of your surroundings. When you finally do, you find true freedom.

We usually think freedom means being allowed to do what we want and go where we choose. Yet this definition of freedom overlooks the fact that *the person who controls and judges you the most is you.* True freedom is not something that can be granted or taken away by another: only we have that power over ourselves.

Freedom is self-acceptance. It is allowing ourselves to be, letting go of the desperate need for approval that makes us adopt uncomfortable social norms in order to fit in. External approval will never be enough as long as we continue craving it, and this is true because of one simple truth: *we do not approve of ourselves.* Because of this, we try to get others to do it for us. But trying to substitute external approval for self-love is like turning up the television to drown out the cries of a baby — a distraction that does nothing to help the situation.

True freedom is freedom from victimhood. It is about taking responsibility for who you are, embracing who you are, and trusting in your own inner voice.

Remember, I do not want you to try to emulate these ways of behaving if you do not feel them. Don't deny your current perception in order to fit into an intellectual idea of the "right way to behave"; instead, expand your consciousness and you will naturally adopt the actions of a creator.

TAKING RESPONSIBILITY FOR OUR CHOICES

Ultimately, being responsible means taking responsibility for ourselves, for the choices we make in every moment.

We really have no idea how powerful we are. We tend to see ourselves as tiny individuals in an enormous world, doing our best to sway the tides that come between us and our desires. Yet there is a truth that can change this perception, destroy the feeling of victimhood, and bring true freedom:

What you focus on grows.

Our focus creates our reality. If we are focused on what is wrong in our lives and our worlds, what are we going to see? What's wrong. Yet if we are focused on the things we love, the things that inspire us and fill us with joy, we start to see the beauty we were so blind to before. You can transform your experience of life in an instant, just by turning your focus inward. Just by bringing your attention deep into yourself instead of getting caught up in the dramas and worries of the world, you can break lifelong patterns of discontent and preoccupation.

So if it's so simple, why don't we do it? I know why: because we don't want to. We don't want to be happy — we'd prefer to fight for what we think should be fixed. We don't want to surrender: we want to win. We don't want to embrace our reality: we want to chase our ideas of how things *should* be, instead of accepting them as they are. Why? Because we are convinced we know best how our lives should be.

Children don't do this. They embrace what they have without question. When I lived on the Colombian coast, the local boys would play football barefoot with coconuts. They weren't moping around thinking, *If only I had some Nike sneakers! Then I could play much better. If only we had a real ball instead of this coconut!* They didn't think like that. They were having so much fun as it was, enjoying what they had.

I am not denying the importance of working toward a better world. I admire any activity that helps unite humanity and improve the quality of life on this planet. Yet if we are focused on what's wrong, even with the intention of making it right, we are perpetuating discontent and nonconformity with what is. Let's focus on what we have achieved, on the wonderful, incredible world we live in and the passionate and inspired individuals who are giving their best to humanity every day. Let's focus on what we can give, on the ways we can lead more joyful, fulfilling lives. Let's focus on being fully present, on knowing ourselves, accepting ourselves, embracing ourselves. Then naturally we will share that love with those around us.

What are you focused on right now? On the frustrations of the past, and the worries of the future? Why not try, just for today, to focus on enjoying each moment, on giving the best you can in each situation that is presented to you?

Discover the power of focus, and in doing so, take responsibility for your own happiness.

HOMEWORK

Today, focus on enjoying every moment. When you find yourself worrying or regretting a past moment, just look up at the sky and laugh at yourself. Think, "Oops, I'm doing it again!" and bring yourself back into the present.

BECOMING A CREATOR: DO YOU HAVE WHAT IT TAKES?

Society manufactures victim-consciousness. The media champions the victim, fighting for the underdog, feeding the idea that we are victims who need to be saved from our oppressors. This mentality is so ingrained in us that it is hard for us to understand that we are not victims. The idea might even offend us; it might seem cruel or lacking in compassion. Yet seeing people as victims is the most debilitating attitude we can have: it holds people in their impotence, denying their ability to change. A compassionate attitude inspires people to greatness, beyond their external situations. I am not suggesting we deny injustice or ignore the needs of the human family; I am suggesting that the most important and lasting service we can give is to heal our own inner victim and, as a result, our perception of victimhood in others.

It takes courage to be a creator. You must stand in your own greatness and take full responsibility for everything that happens in your world, but the rewards are endless: the result is supreme satisfaction, with yourself and with life.

THE GRASS IS ALWAYS GREENER

One classic form of victimhood comes from suffering for what we cannot have. We have become experts at finding what is missing and focusing our energy on it: a surefire way to suck all the happiness out of life. A woman who cannot give birth can forget the positive aspects of her life in her frustration: she might have the perfect partner, conditions to adopt if she wishes, fulfillment in her work, the freedom to travel and pursue her interests. But her rigid idea of *how things should be*, her disappointment with what she cannot have can become her obsession, overshadowing the magic and opportunity present in every moment. The same can happen with any part of life we feel is lacking: the missing soul mate can eclipse the passion we have for our career, or our unemployment can blind us to the support of a loving family. Even the emails in my spam folder reflect our tendency to focus on what is missing: I am constantly bombarded with penis enhancement offers, and (although I don't wish to belittle these difficulties or the feeling of impotence that comes with them) it has become clear to me that a feeling of anatomical shortcoming is just one of many scapegoats we tend to blame for all our stress and frustration. We blame our dissatisfaction on this one thing we cannot change. In doing so, we relinquish our capacity to find joy in all the wonderful things life brings.

VICTIM VS. CREATOR RESPONSES
TO REAL-LIFE SITUATIONS

There are many situations where it is easy to see the difference between a victim response and that of a creator. The following examples can help you become more aware of your own victim attitude and begin to make new choices.

SITUATION OR ATTRIBUTE	VICTIM APPROACH	CREATOR APPROACH
Intimate Relationship	You're not making me happy. I need you to love me in order to feel valuable.	I find joy in giving to you. I want to serve you in being the best you can be, just as I am committed to being the best of myself. I am open to receive your love, and I deserve your love.
Loss	Why do bad things happen to me? I cannot be happy because my external circumstances don't allow me to be. If I had better opportunities I could feel complete or realize my potential.	I embrace the things that happen in my life as opportunities to grow. I trust that even the things I did not want to happen are bringing the best to me. I surrender to what is and flow with whatever comes. My joy lies in embracing and enjoying, not in resisting and complaining.

SITUATION OR ATTRIBUTE	VICTIM APPROACH	CREATOR APPROACH
Lack	I don't have enough time/money/support.	If I am fully present, I realize I have everything I need in each moment. By trusting and flowing, I am open to fully appreciate the abundance that is always flowing toward me.
Giving	I need to take because I don't have enough. People want to take from me, so I must protect what I have.	I am here to serve; it is my joy to give from the abundance I have within. In giving, I am receiving, for I am giving to myself. The more I give, the more I receive.

SITUATION OR ATTRIBUTE	VICTIM APPROACH	CREATOR APPROACH
Trust	In the past, when I have trusted, I have been disappointed. I expect things to go wrong.	Trust comes from trusting. My choice to trust reflects my integrity: it doesn't depend on the external result. If I trust, I win, whatever the outcome, for I am trusting in myself.
Making a "Mistake"	It wasn't my fault. I need to explain to you why it wasn't my fault. I need to convince you of my excuse. I don't take responsibility for my actions.	I am responsible for everything: if I make a mistake, I use it as an opportunity to learn, and make new choices next time. I do not defend; I open to listen so I can evolve.

SITUATION OR ATTRIBUTE	VICTIM APPROACH	CREATOR APPROACH
Friendship	Because I am there for you as a friend, you owe me. I give you so much; you must give to me in return.	I give without conditions, and I am open to receive. I am vulnerable with you, and I listen to what you tell me without resistance, because love does not need a defense.
Recognition	I need to be recognized; I need your approval. If you don't approve, you invalidate me. I cannot value myself if you do not praise me.	I value myself; the integrity of my actions is what makes me fulfilled. If I experience external disagreement, I go inward to see how it makes me feel, to become aware of that within myself. My sense of self-worth is based on my internal experience of consciousness, which does not depend on the shifting opinions of those around me.

SITUATION OR ATTRIBUTE	VICTIM APPROACH	CREATOR APPROACH
Action	Everything feels like a chore. I receive any request with resistance. I cut corners wherever I can out of laziness. Mediocrity marks my actions.	I say yes to everything. Excellence marks my actions, and I find joy in giving the best of myself, always evolving toward more.
Responsibility	I am not responsible for the things that happen to me.	I am responsible for my universe.

Contemplation

- Ask yourself, *How do I attempt to fill an internal hole with external recognition? How do I depend on other people's praise to make up for my own self-criticism?*
- Has anything happened to you recently that you blamed on someone else? Are there areas of your life in which you feel powerless or victimized? Can you change your outlook and take action to make yourself a creator in these areas instead?

CHAPTER TWO

Illusion #2: Comfort Is King

EXPRESSED IN THE BELIEF: *Comfort is always a good thing!*
   The more, the better.
REALITY: *All of life's challenges make us stronger.*

*I*n our society, people view comfort as king. Anything that makes life easier and requires less effort is prized. We have learned to refrain from speaking our truth for fear of conflict and to avoid confronting our fears whenever possible. We have come to value routine over the unknown, and security over spontaneity. Yet often the things that make us uncomfortable — the hard knocks, the disappointments, and the losses — are what challenge us most in our lives. We wish we did not have to weather these storms, yet they are what make us strong. They give us maturity and responsibility, and after all, what better teacher can we have than our own direct experience?

Life becomes stagnant when we remove or avoid its challenges. If a child is spoiled, her parents or servants doing everything for her, when she finally faces the world, she will find herself without the skills to function in society. Similarly, if we overprotect ourselves and try to avoid the inevitable conflicts of life, we may find comfort, but we will not build the skills that lead us toward growth. We may find distraction, but not self-realization.

The story of the Buddha is a perfect example of this. As the prince Siddhartha, he was protected from the world to the point of never seeing the aged or the sick. When he eventually discovered the things that had been hidden from him, he was unprepared for the shock he felt. He then went to the other extreme, committing himself to a life of penance and suffering, before finally finding the "middle path." The extremes of the world are all part of life, and by exaggeratedly protecting our children from these realities, we are not doing them any favors.

How did you grow from a child into a responsible adult? Was it by not making any mistakes? Or was it through learning from the consequences of your actions? Ultimately, we have to go through things ourselves before we fully understand. To flourish and grow as individuals, we must face the world head-on and embrace the losses and disappointments life brings us. Then, instead of perceiving difficult situations as obstacles in our way, we can utilize them as opportunities to grow, to push through our boundaries and expand our horizons.

It is natural to experience ups and downs in life. We are having a human experience, and that entails a wide range of feelings and situations. When we begin to nourish an internal space of security and unconditional love through the expansion of love-consciousness, we start to experience these extremes more freely. We begin to embrace the contrasts of life and find adventure in change and uncertainty. Self-realization is not about living in a permanent blissed-out state where you never feel any emotions. It is about embracing the contrasts of life fully, without fear. When we are rooted in internal freedom, the need to control our circumstances falls away and we can dance unfettered to the varying harmonies of the symphony of life.

COMFORT CHECKLIST

☐ If your body is unhealthy because of excessive comfort, get some exercise.

☐ If your mind is storing resentment because you've been avoiding conflict in order to stay comfortable, go and speak to the person you are avoiding.

☐ If your heart is closed because it seems more comfortable to distract yourself externally than to go inward and release your pain, stop ignoring what's really going on. Be honest with yourself and allow your trapped emotions to be released.

MOVING OUT OF YOUR COMFORT ZONE

Comfort stems from fear of the unknown and fear of failure. We feel safe within its confines, but in reality comfort is a gilded cage barring us from our true greatness. When we're not challenging ourselves to be more, we are settling for mediocrity. We lament what's missing from our lives, but we don't move into action in order to change it. The fear of failure clouds our perception of our full potential. The mind convinces us we are not capable of more, so we stay put.

We cling to comfort because we fear our greatness. It is safer to sit in the shadows than stand in the limelight: there we risk criticism and external judgment. Greatness requires the courage to stand alone and not compromise our truth. It provokes change and causes evolution. Greatness goes out on a limb; it doesn't stick to the status quo. To trust ourselves, to stand in integrity without abandoning ourselves in order to please others — that's greatness.

There is a certain level of collective complacency within society. To break with that and stand alone requires courage, but if we wish to be free from our own inertia, we must take the risk and stop worrying about what other people might think. We must be willing to make what we consider to be mistakes; to try new things and have new experiences; to dare to show ourselves and express ourselves.

If I stand out from the crowd, if I do something noteworthy, I put myself in a place of responsibility. It requires less effort just to sit back and blame my financial situation, my upbringing, or society for not fulfilling my dreams. Yet we are all capable of moving beyond our comfort zone and achieving greatness; in fact, some of the most inspiring and celebrated individuals in history have gone beyond all odds to realize spectacular achievements. They are the ones who said yes when the world said no, the ones who could have used their extreme circumstances as an excuse to achieve nothing, but chose not to.

Michelle Bachelet is an example who has particularly inspired me, a single mother who went through exile and her father's death under torture before becoming the first female president of Chile — as not only a socialist but also an agnostic divorcee in a traditionally Catholic country. Her commitment to the welfare of her people weathered initial public disdain to eventually garner her the highest approval ratings for a Chilean president in the past twenty years; to her country she was as a mother, warm but firm, knowing that her children would thank her later for insisting on doing the right thing.

There was once a ten-year-old boy who had lost his left arm at an early age. He would stand outside the local judo dojo, watching wistfully as the other boys trained. One day the sensei joined him outside.

"Would you like to learn judo?" he asked.

"I'd love to, but I can't," the boy replied, pointing to his missing arm.

The sensei looked at him. "I can teach you judo," he said.

They began classes immediately. In the first class, the sensei taught the boy a simple move and asked him to repeat it over and over to perfection. After three months, the master had refused to teach him any other moves, insisting he practice tirelessly the same move he had learned in his first class.

"Can't we try something new?" the boy asked. "There are so many different moves in judo, and I've only learned one!" But the master was adamant and insisted he continue practicing the same move. Not quite understanding but trusting in his teacher, the boy continued training.

Several months later, the sensei took the boy to his

first tournament. To his surprise, using his single move he won his first two matches with ease. The third was a little harder, but after a while his opponent lost his patience and charged at him; the boy deftly used his one move to win the match. The boy looked in disbelief at his teacher, amazed to find himself in the final round.

His opponent in the final was much bigger and stronger than he was. He was certain he couldn't win, but his master looked on encouragingly, and he shrugged and went into the fight. He had never imagined he would get this far, so what did he have to lose?

The fight was long and intense, his opponent showing no signs of tiring. Yet the boy kept going, waiting for him to drop his guard so he could make his move. Finally he did — just for a moment, but it was enough. He used his move to pin down his opponent, and won the match and the tournament. He was the champion!

The boy rushed to his master in disbelief. "Sensei, how is it possible I won the tournament when I know only one move?"

"Simple," the sensei answered. "You have almost mastered one of the most difficult judo throws. The only known defense for that move is for your opponent to grab your left arm."

Can a black man be president of the United States? Can an open lesbian host a top-rated talk show? Can a nonviolent ascetic liberate a nation from imperial reign? Can a man with severe paralysis inspire scientific minds more than anyone else since Einstein? Can a deaf man write a concerto? Of course they can. So why can't you overcome your self-imposed limitations? We are surrounded by people who have gone beyond mediocrity, even though they had quite valid reasons not to. When we have passion in our hearts, when we are willing to challenge what we are accustomed to and push through our fears, nothing is insurmountable: everything seems possible, and our dreams start to become a reality. When we create our dreams, we become unlimited.

Contemplation

Where are you being comfortable in your life? Where are you sitting back, preferring not to act so as not to rock the boat? Excessive comfort can manifest as physical laziness, overeating, or a general resistance to being proactive or to change, or, more subtly, as a continual avoidance of confrontation, intimacy, or situations that cause you extreme emotions. Observe these places of comfort in your life, and start challenging them. Move out of your comfort zone as much as you can. Walk toward the people who make you feel uncomfortable or insecure, and tell them they do. Then see how that makes you feel. Try new things. Take risks. Dare to be uncomfortable.

You will soon find that any self-abandonment, however "comfortable" it appears, is always ultimately dissatisfying. It leaves you listless, uninspired, and unhappy with yourself. Being direct, honest, and proactive, pushing yourself to be more, and challenging the ideas you have about who you are and what you are capable of seems uncomfortable at times to the mind, but it is infinitely more fulfilling.

CHAPTER THREE

Illusion #3: There Is Not Enough

EXPRESSED IN THE BELIEFS: *I am lacking in something.*
  I must take as much as I can get.
REALITY: *We have everything we could ever want or need.*

The idea that we need something we don't have right now is the root of our discontent. We are never completely satisfied with this moment. Even when we get everything we thought we always wanted, it feels like there is something missing. Why? Because deep down, we feel that we are lacking, that we need something more. And we have become so accustomed to waiting for that something, that nothing is ever enough. The habit of feeling dissatisfied has become almost universal in modern life. This is true for the rich and the poor, for the loners and the social butterflies among us.

How do we break this vicious cycle of unfulfilled desire?

Many spiritual traditions interpret desire as counterproductive, something we must conquer in order to experience realization. Other schools of thought, such as positive thinking, consider the fulfillment of desire to be the goal of our spiritual work. I propose an alternative approach: Embrace desire, so you can see through it.

When we deny a desire, it gets bigger. We all know what we will immediately start thinking about if we are told not to think of an elephant. Similarly, if we're craving a piece of chocolate cake but tell ourselves we shouldn't have one, chocolate cake will crop up in every corner of our minds. Yet it is also true that if we want to experience inner fulfillment, we must learn to transcend the fickle whims of the mind, which fluctuate constantly in an unending cycle of highs and lows, achievements and disappointments, successes and failures.

Spiritual realization is the greatest desire of the heart. Just as an adult is no longer interested in the toys a toddler would find fascinating, a taste of love-consciousness makes other desires pale in comparison. So we find liberation not by denying desire but by discovering our truest, purest desire. Once we do that, then the obsessive and needy desires for external satisfactions naturally lose their power.

Our desires are tinted by the memories stored in our subconscious minds. Women who repeatedly find themselves in abusive relationships often come from violent upbringings, and associate abuse with love. Of course they are not consciously choosing this, but the trauma of past experiences taints their choice of partners. For others, the things we look for in a partner may be the things we felt were missing from our mother's affections. A desire for personal wealth may be motivated by having felt less wealthy than our friends at school, or wanting to prove ourselves to someone we looked up to or even envied. Of course, these are just examples and each of our stories is unique and different, but the important thing here is that we understand that our desires are not rational and because of this they cannot be removed by rational thought. Any attempt to intellectualize our way out of desire will ultimately end in denial; even though intellectually we want to let the desire go, the support system of our personal matrix is controlling us from a deeper level. We can convince ourselves that we really don't need that new car, that soon we will tire of it and be lusting after a newer model, but although we may understand this intellectually, the want that drives the desire does not come from the intellect; it comes from a deeper space, a place where we feel incomplete within ourselves, where we feel that something is lacking. Although we may not succumb to the desire, the craving remains, influencing our life in ways we may not even be aware of: manifesting as other desires or feelings of lack, obsession, or need.

This becomes more evident in extreme situations, such as substance abuse. An alcoholic may be aware of the damage his habit inflicts upon himself and his loved ones yet continue to choose the same destructive behavior. Why? Because although he is aware of the consequences, subconsciously he feels that he deserves no better, and there lies the deeper addiction: to suffering and guilt, an emotional charge that wins over rational thought. He can intellectually remind himself of his responsibilities and of how bad he will feel the next day, but the need to suffer and self-destruct is so strong that it often wins. Love-consciousness is more powerful than our subconscious programmings. When we elevate the vibration of love, feeding that experience, the light of our awareness starts to shine more brightly, and the shadows of our obsessions, fears, and attachments start to fade away. We continue to elevate our consciousness, bit by bit, until the vibration becomes stronger than the programming. We no longer feel that we're lacking anything. Then the situation is reversed. The intellect is no longer in control. It becomes a servant of love-consciousness, a tool that love-consciousness can use to interact with the world.

When you find yourself obsessed with a desire, something you feel incomplete without, stop for a moment. Close your eyes and take your attention inward. Ask yourself, *What is missing in this moment?* Bring your awareness fully into the present, experiencing this moment and the sensations it brings in all their intensity. Go deeper, beneath the thoughts and sensations: what lies there? You may not feel it at first, but as you become more accustomed to taking your awareness beyond the surface level of perception, you will discover the joyful fullness of being that is always present, always complete. The experience of love-consciousness is so profound and fulfilling that you will soon become addicted to it, because you will realize that it is the only thing that can complete you. This is the best addiction you can have, for it produces no craving and its supply never runs out.

There is nothing wrong with desire; the trick is to *desire without attachment.* What really matters is that you be in each moment. Be present, and be willing to let go of the attachment to how things need to look. If you focus on being instead of having, on experiencing this moment to the fullest instead of on the object of your desire, everything comes. It comes by itself.

Before, things had to look a certain way for me. In order to experience joy, I had to receive something specific from the outside: recognition, material gain, romantic love, attention. I had to win: I had to be the best at what I did. If not, there was no joy. Now that has changed, and you know what left with it? The suffering. That doesn't mean that I no longer have goals or projects; it just means that my fulfillment no longer depends on their outcome. Now I put all my passion into creating and exploring my pursuits, but if something doesn't turn out as planned, I no longer suffer.

The world we live in is meant for us to love it. It is designed for us to experience it to the fullest, in our own unique and perfect expression. Let's celebrate life, explore our dreams and aspirations, and at the same time cultivate an inner experience that takes us beyond them, to establish a space of stability and self-acceptance from which we can watch the magic of existence unfold.

NEED WITHIN RELATIONSHIPS

Have you ever noticed that within relationships many of us feel a constant need to test our partners? It doesn't matter what we receive; we always push for more: more commitment, more love, more affection — nothing ever seems to be enough. This tendency, too, stems from a deep feeling of lack and of being unworthy of love. And when our partners invariably fail to fulfill our ever-changing needs, we become resentful within the reality we have created: instead of giving praise, love, and gratitude, we constantly complain about what's not present.

This happens not only with our partners but with our bosses and colleagues, our friends and relatives as well. The root of dissatisfaction in any relationship is the same: we are not doing things unconditionally; we are doing them in order to receive approval or compensation. This is contractual love. Instead of giving, we are looking for what we can take. How do we resolve this? By inverting our perception:

I am what I give, not what I take.

When I become the source of joy and love, I only give in my interactions with others. I don't need any confirmation that I am worthy of love. If I start to give recognition, if I start to appreciate, if I become the source of love and find internal achievement, polishing my behaviors and attitudes in every moment, I become a joyous being, a happy being, a being that inspires others to give more and create more. As a consequence, I rise above my feeling of lack and feel a sense of abundance that I want to share with others. And so, ever joyful, I give and give.

Don't focus on what's missing: focus on what you can give — where you can give praise, where you can give love. This will elevate your being to a place of joy.

That which enlivens the hearts of others makes yours glow. Maybe you find passion for life by standing on a freezing street corner handing out soup. Or it could be through picking up litter on the side of the road, helping those in need, or just being there for someone who could use a compassionate ear. Engage with your environment, and everywhere you look you will start to see opportunities to give.

I am what I give, not what I take.

Love-consciousness gives with infectious enthusiasm; it sparks and inspires. This is quite different from giving because we feel obligated to based on what we think society expects of us. This giving comes from joy, from the perception of unity: *I am that, therefore I give to that. I see where I can serve, where I can be more, how I can give more to others.* It comes from a place of completion, not from the need of approval.

It doesn't matter what you're giving as long as you're giving. When I was a child, I used to fill an old jar with water and rose petals, preparing what I envisioned as the sweetest rose perfume for my mother. In reality the sodden old petals probably didn't smell like much, and the stagnant water might have been better suited for tadpoles, but my mother always received it with delight! It was the giving that connected our hearts, not the object itself. This is the nature of true giving: childlike, spontaneous, joyful.

GIVING AND RECEIVING

The disparity between how much we think we give and how much we deem we get in return is often the cause of conflict in relationships. There is almost always one who gives, gives, gives and then is disappointed when nothing comes in return, and another who takes, takes, takes but cannot truly appreciate what they are receiving. Resentment ensues, and what began as a passionate and committed relationship grinds to an abrupt and unexpected halt. In some cases, people spend years bearing this resentment, both parties accumulating an exhaustive list of reproaches as thick as a phonebook.

Those who give while expecting something in return give with condition. Ultimately, they feel that they don't deserve love — that old, forgotten feeling still lies there deep down, covered in resentment and demanding retribution.

In the other half of the equation are those who don't have the capacity to give, those who only take from others. For them, nothing is ever enough. They are never satisfied. They take, but they cannot *receive*.

Both parties must find love within, and when they discover it, the fear of giving dissolves. With it goes the fear of receiving. Then a new cycle is formed, one that starts with giving, always giving, unconditionally. As a consequence, they begin to truly receive: everything comes to them, flowing in an eternal circle of unbounded, unconditional love, which knows only to share and to flow.

If you focus on giving unconditionally, from the endless source of love that lies within, you will find that your internal experience does not diminish and your love never runs out. From this pure, clean form of giving — a giving that comes from healing, from a full, joyful present, not from entanglement in a past still kicking and screaming for the injustices it has faced — you will realize that in giving you are not losing; that in reality, when you give from a place of joy, you are giving to yourself.

Contemplation

- In what area or areas of your life are you always wanting more? It could be food, alcohol or drugs, fashionable clothing, fancy cars, money, love, or more recognition or achievement at work. By becoming aware of these areas, you can start to deactivate their power: when you feel the outward pull that takes your attention away from yourself and fixes it on the object of your desire, reverse that energetic movement by taking your attention deep within. Close your eyes, center your awareness in your heart, and ask yourself, *What am I feeling in this moment?* When your cravings are activated, the feeling of lack, anxiety, or internal emptiness that drives them will be more evident than ever, if you take the time to go inward and listen. Allow yourself to feel this charge, and bit by bit, it will dissipate. If you do this every time you feel the need for something external, you will soon be free of the root of your craving.

- The next time you're longing for something from someone in your life, give them that thing instead. Do you feel that your boss never acknowledges your performance at work? Praise your boss or another coworker when they do something that makes your job easier. Feel that your partner doesn't open up to you? Be more vulnerable yourself. When you give what you feel is missing, you become aware of the unlimited source (of approval, attention, love, support) that lies within you, and in doing so you begin to depend less on receiving things from an external source.

- When was the last time you gave without expecting anything in return? Brainstorm ways in which you could give selflessly this week — clean up litter in your neighborhood, volunteer at a local animal shelter, clean out your cupboards and donate food to a homeless shelter. Then actually *do* at least one of these acts of giving. Afterward, notice how you feel: you will probably feel that you have gained more than you have given away.

CHAPTER FOUR

Illusion #4: Being Passive Protects Me from Making Mistakes

EXPRESSED IN THE BELIEFS: *I prefer to sit back when action is required, so as not to risk making a mistake. If I do nothing, things will work themselves out.*

REALITY: *Strength comes from taking action in our lives.*

*M*any people prefer to sit around doing nothing than to take action in their lives. They avoid taking responsibility. They don't want to make decisions. They prefer to be led blindly into a future they won't want to confront anyway, a future that they believe will ultimately end in resentment and disillusionment. Their passivity reflects — and perpetuates — their lack of passion in life.

Some stay in unfulfilling jobs for decades, complaining to themselves every night about how much they hate their boss or how demeaning the work is. Others remain in abusive relationships, enduring beatings and beratings year after year, believing it's their lot in life. And millions of people throughout the Western world become more and more obese, watching TV as they mindlessly snack on junk food. Their breathing becomes chronically labored, their blood pressure rises, and their joints give out on them, leaving them in chronic pain.

They completely forget the joy of movement. And still they sit passively by.

Of course, these are extreme examples. Much more common are the people who reach a place of relative comfort in life and settle into it at the expense of pursuing their dreams and passions. This reminds me of a friend of mine. She had one of the most extraordinary voices I had ever heard and one of the most beautiful faces I had ever seen. She had a personality, looks, and talent destined for stardom and a dream of becoming a world-famous singer. She even had the opportunity to travel around the world in the mid-seventies as a support singer for one of the most successful singer-songwriters of her time. When she returned, she was poised for stardom, yet she let the new opportunities slip away: instead of embracing her incredible gift, she did everything possible to destroy it. Her self-esteem was chronically low, and she covered this up with extreme addictions. She drank heavily, consumed large amounts of drugs, and smoked to the point that she destroyed her voice completely. Instead of pursuing her passion, she chose to stay at home drinking and to waste away the hours at slot machines. On the way back from one of her drunken escapades, she fell off her bike and badly damaged her face. She never believed she deserved what she had, and instead of achieving greatness, she remained comfortable within her dysfunction.

Passivity can also take the form of stopping at life's unexpected roadblocks without trying to find a way around them. In such situations it is useful to remember the adage "Where there is a will, there is a way." A perfect example of the importance of taking action at times like this happened recently during my first European tour.

While visiting Amsterdam, we found ourselves in the midst of chaos as a volcano erupted in Iceland, covering most of Europe with a cloud of ash. With hundreds of flights canceled and thousands of tourists suddenly stranded, it seemed we would never make the next stop on our tour — Vienna, where I planned to see the legendary Lipizzaner stallions of the Spanish Riding School, a dream I had held since early childhood. After much juggling and conferring, a lifesaving ticket officer at the Amsterdam Central Station mapped out a complex route, with several changes that would get us there on time. Everything went as planned, but what we hadn't expected (our knowledge of volcanic eruptions at the time was minimal) was that the next stop on our tour would also be affected, as the ash continued to do its damage.

Getting to the next destination was much more urgent — I had a live interview with CNN scheduled in Madrid — and we had much farther to travel. However, the main obstacle was not the distance but the fact that after crossing Switzerland we had to pass through France. The perennial French train strike was, of course, in effect (the convictions of the strikers not to be hampered by anything as insignificant as a giant cloud of volcanic ash causing an unprecedented demand for train travel). Our ticket went via Lyon and then Nîmes, and then trailed off into a series of possible routes that would depend on the erratic temperament of the striking staff and the constantly shifting timetables of overcrowded vehicles.

After rushing to catch a train in Lyon that was so crowded we couldn't find a seat and had to join the fifteen other people cramped between the WC and the carriage door, perched atop our suitcases and politely contorting ourselves to one side so passengers could tiptoe past us on their way to the bathroom, we were finally ejected in Nîmes only to ensconce ourselves in another similarly full-to-bursting carriage, rivaling any Tokyo subway car. We eventually found ourselves in Perpignan, where we traipsed across town following the pied-piper line of forlorn tourists from one station to the other, only to find that there were no more trains going anywhere near Spain for the rest of the day. Still 500 miles from Madrid but determined to arrive in time for the interview, we finally gave in and took a cab. The expense and hassle notwithstanding, we made the interview, and the rest of our visit to Spain went wonderfully.

A year later, another volcano began belching out ash, this time much closer to home, in Chile. For us, this eruption co-incided with a trip from Mexico to a seminar in Buenos Aires, Argentina. When we arrived in Chile, our connecting flight had been canceled, and after several hours of waiting and hop-ing that another flight would become available, we decided to try the land route while we still had the chance of arriving on time for our event. A friend drove us from the airport to the Argentinean border, where we crossed on foot amid magnifi-cent snowy peaks, forgetting the cold as we stood in wonder, mesmerized by the magical beauty of the Andes. We were met on the other side by another friend who had come to collect us from the nearby city of Mendoza. We arrived at the Mendoza airport just in time to find that the last flight to Buenos Aires had been canceled. Again, we hopped in a cab, to brave the remaining 700 miles. The seminar was due to start the next morning at ten. We arrived at nine and had just enough time to jump in the shower before the event began. Three days later, we took the whole trip back again, as the ash had still not subsided!

In these circumstances, if we had accepted the travel limitations at face value, we would have remained stuck where we didn't want to be, moping about all our foiled plans and disappointing thousands of people who had signed up to learn the Isha System, not to mention missing out on a grand adventure. When we embrace what life brings and take action to change our situation, we can have fun along the way, even when the journey takes much longer than expected!

Passivity vs. Surrender

A master was traveling through the desert with one of his disciples. When night fell, they stopped and put up their tent to sleep. The disciple's job was to tie up the camel, but he didn't bother and just left the camel loose outside the tent. He sat down to meditate and said to the universe, "I trust that everything is perfect: you take care of the camel!" With that, he fell asleep.

In the morning when he awoke, the camel was nowhere to be seen. It might have been stolen, it might have escaped — anything could have happened!

The master asked his disciple, "What happened? Where is the camel?!"

"I don't know," replied the disciple. "Ask the universe — I very clearly told it to take care of him for me. You always teach me to trust in the perfection of the universe, and so I trusted. Now don't blame me!"

> *The master said, "Trust in the universe, but first, tie up your camel!"*

As you tread the path of awakening, don't confuse surrender with passivity. Don't think that embracing the moment and accepting what comes means just sitting around and waiting for everything to fall from the sky. Life doesn't work like that. You need to put things into motion. Just hanging around waiting generates inertia and stagnation. Lots of people sit in that space of passivity. Then, when nothing happens, they feel like victims because their expectations have not been fulfilled.

Surrender and passivity are worlds apart. Surrender is the action of trusting in the creative force of the universe. It embraces the moment with joy, rejoicing in its fullness. Surrender is vibrant, active, engaging, and trusting. Passivity is complacent, disillusioned, resentful, and dissatisfied. Surrender comes from love and trust, while passivity stems from bitterness and disappointment. It doesn't let go and flow with what comes; it stems from a place of resignation.

Elizabeth, my bulldog, is a wonderful example of surrender to life. The first time I laid eyes on her, in a pet shop in Chile, she stole my heart. She was an undernourished puppy, physically stunted and covered in warts. The poor thing had been caged in the store for four months; no one would buy her because she was so small for her age. I was shocked to hear she had been living like that for so long, and although I had not been planning on getting another dog (I already had seven!) she was impossible for me to resist.

Elizabeth embraces her reality completely, as all dogs do. They don't sit there wondering if their lives could be different; they have an innate ability to enjoy life with exuberance and without questioning. This is a gift that we humans could learn a lot from. With all the passive wallowing that clouds our days, inhibiting our ability to truly enjoy what is in front of us, our capacity to find true happiness is greatly diminished. Our inability to embrace the beauty of our present reality, combined with our reluctance to take steps to change the things that aren't working, holds us in discontent. But not for Elizabeth! She embraces everything with loving acceptance, and I believe that this surrender is what brought her into my life. Because she surrendered to the reality of her situation in that pet store, now she experiences the other extreme: she lives in the lap of luxury, adored and pampered to her heart's content. She is the most loving and affectionate dog I have ever had; she is quite happy to fall asleep on top of Mummy, her slobbery chops resting on my shoulder.

We get what we give in life. If we face unpleasant circumstances with impotent resentment and inaction, those circumstances will only get worse. Yet if we can learn to accept the hardships with surrender and trust — trust that everything is bringing us toward a greater freedom that we cannot yet conceive in its entirety — while also taking steps to better our situation, maybe, just maybe, we can transform our suffering into an opportunity for growth.

Do what has to be done. Don't ignore your reality. Then, when you've done all you can, let go and trust in the universe: it knows very well what it is doing.

Contemplation

- Where in your life are you being passive? There are many different areas of our lives where we abandon ourselves and don't stand in our power.

- Do you speak your truth with your partner, or do you adapt your responses to avoid conflict? Many of us expect our partners to know what we are feeling without our having to tell them. Then we get resentful when they don't guess!

- Do you avoid making decisions for fear of making a mistake? It can feel safer to be passive and do nothing, but missing the opportunities life presents you will never leave you satisfied. Take a risk — be willing to make a mistake! Then, if you don't like the result, you will know to do things differently next time.

- Do you habitually postpone things you could (or should) do now? Procrastination is the hallmark of passivity, and it comes from a lack of trust in your own inner voice. Listen to your heart, not the doubts of the head: the heart always knows which decision will lead to more love.

CHAPTER FIVE

Illusion #5: Discrimination Is Acceptable, for Certain People and Things Are Better Than Others

EXPRESSED IN THE BELIEF: *Certain aspects of this world are in some way imperfect or better or worse than others.*
REALITY: *All of creation is worthy of love.*

*D*iscrimination comes from a resistance to embracing anything outside of our own personal boxes. We discriminate against the unfamiliar, against that which we do not identify with, that which falls outside our theology, our ideas. In order to define ourselves as individuals, we must have personalities. Within those personalities we structure belief systems, but as soon as we start to identify with those belief systems, we must defend them, for they now define who we are. As we become love-consciousness, we realize that our belief systems are simply ideas we have cultivated throughout our lives. We start to embrace new perspectives with an open mind instead of an automatic rejection. When we become the love, we embody everything. When we limit ourselves to our personalities and belief systems, there is no room in our boxes for anything else.

How many of our opinions are truly our own? When we

get down to it, very few of our convictions come from our direct experience; most we have adopted from our families and society in general. What is right in one part of the world might be considered wrong in another. What one generation rejects, another may embrace. Having multiple wives in some cultures is illegal; in others it is a sign of wealth. Just because an opinion is widespread doesn't make it valid — there was a time when everyone thought the sun revolved around the Earth. If you are looking for it, you can find validation for pretty much any opinion you have. The illusion will always confirm your fears; it works as an impartial mirror, reflecting back whatever you are focused on. If I have a fear or judgment, it will be easy to find external support that will justify my prejudice.

Prejudice means always going to war. Prejudice means always defending an idea and justifying our discrimination with the excuse of the higher good — *for the betterment of humanity, the will of god*. "Isms" are always "good-isms" in the eyes of the self-righteous.

Historically, we have dropped bombs, fought, and slaughtered in order to protect our beliefs. Let's not do that anymore. Every time we fight for an opinion, even within our immediate family, we are creating our own mini-war. The conflict we perceive in the world is just a manifestation of our own internal violence. As we start to choose joy, let's learn to love the world's duality and other people's differences, knowing that they are aspects of ourselves. Let's find the lightness of laughter and write a new story for the history books to come.

Nature, with its infinite number of species, colors, and forms, embraces diversity. Nature denies no aspect of itself; the beauty of its landscapes lies in their contrast and variance.

Like nature, love also celebrates the beauty of diversity. Instead of perceiving anything different as a threat, love shuts out no voice.

All aspects of creation serve. Destruction instigates rebirth. The world dances from torment to calm in the ebb and flow of evolution. With each change the world is reborn in a higher vibration, strengthening the values of joy and love, breaking free of the density of fear.

My grandmother was always very fixed in her ways. She had lived through the Great Depression, and even after moving to an abundant life in Australia's booming economy, she was accustomed to the idea of lack. She would scrimp and save, happily walking a few extra kilometers just to save a few pennies on a bunch of bananas. Her conditioning dictated her actions, and she never stopped to question its relevance to her current reality; her actions were robotic, as were her opinions and ideas.

Because my grandmother had experienced two world wars, she was automatically prejudiced against Germans and Japanese. On both sides of the house I grew up in, our neighbors were German. Additionally, my mother used to teach English to Japanese students. My grandmother, who lived with my family as I grew up, would grumble her prejudices under her breath, maintaining her opinion as something of great value. Interestingly, her opinions didn't affect how she related to our foreign neighbors. The prejudice was actually just an idea in her head! She embraced these people with genuine warmth and acceptance, as she would any other human, even as she kept insisting that the Germans and Japanese were bad people.

My mother rebelled against my grandmother's prejudices, doing everything possible to be open-minded — religiously, politically, and ethnically — by going to great lengths to teach and serve all the minority groups in her world. In reaction to the opinions of your parents, maybe you, too, have gone to the other extreme on certain issues. Your vehement beliefs may seem more justified than whatever you judged in your parents' prejudices, but as long as you are holding a position, you are still discriminating. You may have adopted what you perceive as more evolved beliefs, yet they are still beliefs. If in order for you to be right, someone has to be wrong, you are living in prejudice.

Are your robotic responses really actions of abundance and love, or are they just a programming that keeps you in a place of isolation, perceiving a world steeped in limitation? Observe yourself and become aware of where you shut out the world: every *no* builds a new wall, but every *yes* opens a new possibility.

It is often easier to see discrimination in others than to see it in ourselves. Prejudice is magnified on the global stage as war, racism, religious extremism, and social inequality. We can campaign to change these aspects of humanity, but the most effective way to transform them is to become aware of them in ourselves and make the change within. You may not be racist or classist or sexist per se, but you can find places within yourself where you discriminate. It might be by comparing your job with someone else's or judging other people's level

> *Every* no *builds a new wall, but every* yes *opens a new possibility.*

of intelligence. Even if it's far subtler than overt oppression, it is still discrimination. By making the change within ourselves, we can start to take responsibility for the things we wish to change in the world. By bringing the focus inward, coming back to ourselves, we can transform the world from within.

Contemplation

In what areas are you prejudiced toward other people, places, or things? Maybe you look down on the people who bag your groceries, or perhaps you turn up your nose at a particular type of food. On the other hand, maybe you put certain people or things on a pedestal, respecting or valuing them more than others.

Pay attention to the thoughts you have as you go through your days, noticing the areas where you discriminate. Ask yourself, *Are these my beliefs, or are they the beliefs of my parents, my grandparents, or my culture?* Can you release them and open your heart to the things you've been shutting out?

Question every aspect of your personality. Look at it carefully and ask yourself, *Is this my reality? Does this serve? Or are these prejudices keeping me trapped in a box, limiting my vision?*

Don't scrutinize yourself from a place of severity. Instead, joyfully become aware of your behaviors, and allow them to evaporate like water that forms clouds to later fall as rain, transformed as a nourishing and inclusive embrace of the world.

CHAPTER SIX

Illusion #6: I Am Separate

EXPRESSED IN THE BELIEF: *I am a small, separate being, separate from you and from everyone else.*
REALITY: *We are all one.*

We perceive separation everywhere in our world, from the existence of a hundred billion different galaxies right down to the discrete quarks and electrons of the subatomic level. In addition to the separate entities we perceive in nature, we have come to experience separation from others, in the form of judgments condemning certain aspects of our world as wrong. We may feel separate from a whole group of people due to their social status, political beliefs, nationality, or religion; we may also feel separate from an individual: a parent or other relative, a colleague, or someone who we feel has done us wrong in some way. We then try to avoid this person or group of people. We distance ourselves from them and, on a subtle level, blame them for our discontent.

When we perceive separation externally, we don't stop to consider that it could have something to do with our internal experience. Imagine for a moment that your world is a big mirror, reflecting all your likes and dislikes; so what you disdain in others really comes from inside you. Instead of shunning others and making your aversion about them, start to take responsibility and make it about *you*. I'm talking not about chastising or blaming yourself for your feelings toward the outside world but about going inside and finding that thing you feel separate from within.

If I see separation, I must walk toward it. This is how separation is healed: by bridging the gap, moving closer. Walking away only widens the breach. As soon as I turn a blind eye, negating something on the outside, I am distancing myself. I am denying an aspect of myself, bolstering the distinction between "me" and "them."

Usually, when we feel separate from someone or something in our world, we segregate into different groups, different factions, different likes and dislikes. A classic example of this was the separation of the Church of England from the Roman Catholic Church in the sixteenth century. The separation came about because King Henry VIII sought the annulment of his marriage to his Catholic wife, Catherine of Aragon. The pope refused to grant the annulment, so the king instead appealed to the highest church official in England, the Archbishop of Canterbury. The archbishop granted the annulment, thereby alienating the Catholic Church and laying the groundwork for the establishment of a new church, the Church of England. This is an extreme example of how we change groups or alliances in order to have our own way. By continuing to separate, we reinforce the labels we put on ourselves and others by joining with people who confirm our opinion. With time, these groups become increasingly smaller, as they splinter off into more specific definitions of "us" and "them": every time there is a disagreement or someone doesn't accept our convictions within the group, we remove them from our circle. If we're not careful, we cut out so many aspects of our universe that we end up with only the cat and the television for company. This inner attitude, taken to the extreme, defines allies and enemies; it is the attitude that starts wars, that says, "I am separate from totality."

Embrace your world instead of pushing it away. Reach out and give it a great big hug. Within that embrace, bring it all back to your heart. Hold it close and realize that when you are loving it, you are loving everything.

When you feel separate from your loved ones, walk toward them and speak your truth. Be transparent; open your heart. We think that if we speak our truth we will push away the people we love, but the opposite is true. When we speak our truth we open up a flow from heart to heart, allowing us to heal whatever anguish or separation, injustice or victimization we are perceiving in that moment. If you practice this within your immediate circle, before long you will start extending this embrace to the rest of humanity.

THE EGO:
HEALING THE SEPARATION FROM SELF

In modern spirituality, there is a lot of talk about the ego. I don't focus much on the ego, as I have seen many people get caught in the struggle of fighting against it or trying to destroy it. This comes from a common misconception: the idea that the ego is inherently bad or even evil. This in turn feeds the belief in separation, separation from self.

There is nothing wrong with the ego. It is just a protection. The ego comprises the individual persona, the masks and defenses we use to hide our insecurity. In order to explain this, I often use the following analogy:

Imagine that you are an egg. Inside you is a baby eagle. This eagle represents love-consciousness, your true self, your full potential. Yet you don't know that this eagle exists; for now, you are just an egg. The shell represents the ego. The function of the eggshell is to protect that which is not yet mature, to shield the baby eagle from the world until it is ready. This shell might present itself as false pride or arrogance, as insecurity or feigned humility. It is the voice that tells you there is something wrong with you, that you should be different. It is the voice that is always pulling you down, keeping you small, doubting, mistrusting, worrying. Is there something wrong with the eggshell? No. It's just doing its job, providing protection until the eagle has grown strong. When the baby eagle is big enough, it starts to chip away at the shell. The more it is exposed to the light, the faster the shell falls, because with each new chink, the eagle becomes more aware of a reality far greater than anything it has ever known, and so its desire to break free of its constraints grows. When it finally breaks free, the light rushes in to embrace it from every angle as it basks in the blazing glory of its new kingdom. Spreading its wings, it knows it is no longer the cramped smallness of the egg; it is the king of the sky.

In your journey toward awakening, don't try to destroy the ego or fight against it: in doing so you only feed separation.

Instead, focus on cultivating the majestic eagle within. When your consciousness has matured, the ego will fall away naturally, without any effort on your part, because it will no longer have anything left to protect.

THE IDEAL IDEOLOGY

There are so many ideologies in the world. Some of them are beautiful and some are destructive. Some are creative and others are repressive. Some we might wish to apply and others don't appeal to us, but they all have one thing in common: they are all just ideas (hence the root of the word: *ide*-ology).

In our search to feel safe and define our identities, we attach ourselves to one idea after another. We enclose ourselves into one rigid box after another. Love-consciousness is a room without walls. It has no enclosure, no opinions, just a constant openness to evolution, an unwavering focus on the expansion of love. Its expansion, its vibration, its joy are endless and eternal.

Some ideologies are based in love-consciousness, but if they're insistent — *it has to be like this* — they become oppressive. This is not the behavior of love-consciousness. Love-consciousness does not segregate. It embraces everything and within that embrace moves joyfully toward a higher vibration of love. That which is immature, that which no longer serves, it discards naturally in its constant evolution toward greater awareness, or unity. This is not about denying the things we perceive as negative within the world — like war, famine, or discrimination — or separating ourselves and focusing on what we wish to eliminate. It is about contributing to what we want to see more of — peace, freedom, acceptance.

Don't make one particular idea special. The only thing special, the only thing important, is the joy of being; that peace, that love, growing and moving in ever-expanding waves, the silent witness of an evolving world.

With time, I have found that there is a common core that moves us all, regardless of nationality or creed: love. All religions agree that god is love. The form in which this wisdom is presented may change, and the trappings surrounding this truth may differ, but this core truth is common to all faiths. In the arms of union, we see one being, one love. It is the same in the nun and the atheist, the rabbi and the agnostic, because all ultimately is love. Quantum physics can prove our oneness, though it cannot explain it; it is the ultimate experience, impossible to understand, impossible to deny.

SAVING THE PLANET:
OUR SEPARATION FROM THE WORLD

As global concern for the environment rises, I observe how we face this problem in the same way we do most situations in our lives: we want to fix something that we perceive as terribly wrong. When this happens we look for someone to blame, but in doing so, we sidestep taking responsibility. How do we take responsibility for something like environmental destruction — something that seems so huge and so unrelated to our own actions? I am not downplaying the positive effects of making greener choices or reducing your footprint, but I am talking about going inward, to heal the root causes of destructive behavior within ourselves.

We have so many judgments about what's happening in the world: the destruction of the rain forests, the poisoning of the oceans, oil spills, tribal peoples killing gorillas in order to make money to live — the list goes on and on. Obviously we would like to change these things, but we need to ask ourselves what is at the root of these behaviors. Greed. Lack. Separation. We feel as though there is not enough — not enough natural resources, not enough money, not enough work being done — but although these seem like national and even global problems, this feeling of lack stems from our inner state, our own personal feeling of incompletion. If I feel unfulfilled, I experience need. Until I feel whole, this need will influence my actions, my responses. My giving will not be inclusive; it will not be unconditional. When we find internal abundance, however, we start to transform everything into that abundance. If I'm abundant, I don't let an aspect of myself starve. If I'm abundant, I don't go and burn down the rain forest. If I'm abundant, I don't throw poison into the ocean. So I become that abundance, and because love-consciousness lives in union, as it elevates it affects all aspects of duality. Everything becomes that abundance.

There was once a scientist who was obsessed with finding a way to heal the world. He came up with potions and theories, new inventions and discoveries, trying tirelessly to find the solution. One day, his four-year-old son came into his laboratory.

"What are you doing, Daddy?" he asked.

Distractedly, his father responded, "I'm trying to find a way to heal the world."

The boy was excited. "Really, Daddy? Can I help? I want to save the world! Please, please, tell me what I can do!"

Smiling at the boy's naïveté, the scientist ripped a photo of the world out of a magazine. He tore it into tiny pieces and handed them to the boy.

"Here," he said, "go and fix that."

The boy ran off excitedly, and his father returned to his experiments, knowing that his son, who had no idea what the world looked like, would be entertained for hours with the puzzle.

Five minutes later, the boy returned with the picture of the world perfectly reassembled. His father stared in amazement.

"How did you manage that? You don't even know what the world looks like!"

"That's true, Daddy," said the boy. "I don't know what the world looks like, but you took this picture out of a magazine, and on the back there was a picture of a man. When I fixed the man, I healed the world!"

Let's stop pointing the finger, playing the blame game. Let's start going inward, and when something bothers us, ask, *Where is that within myself? How can I heal that within myself?* We cannot single-handedly change the world, but we can change ourselves, and that, my dear friend, is the most exciting, challenging, and incredible adventure we can ever embark upon.

Contemplation

Make a list of the people you feel separate from. This might include close friends or family members. Try moving toward them, explaining that you want to heal the separation you feel. Be vulnerable. Speak your truth and listen to what they feel: normally when there is a feeling of separation on one side, there is also separation on the other. Don't get caught up in the blame game. Focus on releasing your feelings, speaking your truth, irrespective of the reaction people may have. If they feel offended, instead of reacting to their response or trying to defend yourself, go inward and ask yourself, *How does it make me feel when they react in that way?* If you take everything back in and use it to heal, the situation will become an opportunity for growth instead of ending in an argument.

CHAPTER SEVEN

Illusion #7: I Am a Sinner and I Should Atone for My Sins

EXPRESSED IN THE BELIEFS: *I am capable of sin; I am capable of making a mistake. There is something inherently wrong with me or an aspect of me.*

REALITY: *Unconscious or fear-based behaviors are a natural part of being human, but we have the power to move beyond them.*

"*F*orgive them, Father, for they know not what they do" (Luke 23:34). This is one of my favorite Bible passages. The way I see it, Jesus is saying that we are not conscious of our actions. Out of ignorance, we choose behaviors based in addiction, pride, and greed — behaviors based in fear.

In reality, the forgiveness spoken of in this passage has already been granted: love-consciousness embraces every aspect of life and fully understands the delusions of human unconsciousness. These delusions could be called "sins," although not in the traditional sense of the word. The conventional conception is that sin is essentially evil behavior, something intrinsically wrong or ungodly. Enlightenment sees no inherent evil, and so the concept of sin as we know it is nonsensical; however, love-consciousness does denote specific uplifting actions, as opposed to fear-based behaviors.

The Seven Deadly Sins

Fear-based behaviors are described quite clearly in the seven deadly sins, although again, not as they were traditionally interpreted. Instead of "seven deadly sins" I think a better name would be "seven aspects of unconscious behavior." They are not essentially bad, and we all experience them to some extent in our lives.

Let's have a look at the seven deadly sins and how they transform in the light of love-consciousness.

Lust

Sex is a perfectly natural, joyful expression of life. To feel passion and sexual attraction is an inherent part of our humanity. Lust becomes an addictive behavior when sex becomes an escape, an obsessive distraction to keep us from being with ourselves. Making love is about sharing; it is about giving and receiving, intimacy and vulnerability. When sex is just about taking, satisfying a need, it becomes an addiction. Don't deny your desire; repression only increases the pressure, and there will come a time when you can ignore it no longer. Instead, focus on cultivating the inner fullness that will truly complete you and that is ultimately much more satisfying than fleeting physical pleasure. Then your sexuality will become a sharing of that fullness: it will be joyful, innocent, and transparent instead of needy and frantic.

Gluttony

Overeating is another common habit that we use to avoid ourselves. Essentially, we have learned to use food to repress our emotions. When we do so, eating is no longer about nourishing our bodies, and so our eating habits become unconscious. Instead of eating what the body wants, we eat what our anxiety wants. Anxiety is not hunger — it is important to become aware of the difference in order to heal a destructive relationship with food. When you catch yourself reaching for the fridge, stop for a moment. Go inward and listen to your body. Are you really hungry, or are you just agitated? Give yourself a minute to be with what you're feeling, to get to know it better. You might find that you are not really hungry at all, that you are feeling emotions you hadn't given yourself the time to identify. If you allow yourself to feel them, you will find that the craving for food will begin to subside. With time, you will become more aware of what your body really wants. This is a great step toward love of self.

Greed

Greed is never satisfied. No matter what greed achieves, it is never enough. There is always something more to acquire. Got the car of your dreams? Now you need two. Why are we always waiting for something more?

Most of us spend our entire lives waiting. It has become such a habit that even when the things we are waiting for (the promotion, the marriage, the children) finally arrive, we are incapable of enjoying them in their entirety — we are too busy waiting for something else (retirement, the vacation, the divorce). This is because we don't really know what we want. Greed tells us we want things, but in reality we want to feel satisfied. Greed tells us we want something that is coming in the future, but in actual fact we just don't want to confront our reality, here and now. This moment is the only thing we ever have. The rest is speculation and illusion. We are conditioned with the saying that "good things come to those who wait," but if we are incapable of embracing the perfection of this moment, we are incapable of enjoying life. In reality, it doesn't matter how much we achieve materially; if our greed keeps us locked in the need for more, our wealth will bring us nothing but a more expensive form of misery!

On my journey as a spiritual teacher, I have taught people from many different walks of life, including the rich and famous. Of course they have material freedom, but they have not found fulfillment. We only have to look at our celebrities to see that material wealth does not bring happiness — the countless cases of celebrity depression, substance abuse, and broken relationships are well known to us all.

Material wealth is overrated. I'm not saying there is anything wrong with it; it's just never enough. We live our lives as if we are in a race, chasing the proverbial carrot into infinity. We are always trying to get somewhere — if not a physical place, then at least an emotional or mental one. Beneath it all is the desire to be anywhere but here.

What is so bad about what we have already? When we are truly present, we realize that the answer is…nothing. We realize that in reality we are not running toward happiness; we are running away from ourselves. For this is the crux of the matter: that which we cannot bear to face in this moment is our own dissatisfaction. The hole within ourselves, the feeling of incompletion is what we are avoiding so persistently. The trouble is, it doesn't matter where you go; there you will be.

We might dream of the peace and tranquility of a tropical

island, but like Tom Hanks in *Cast Away*, even in a perfect paradise we will have to confront ourselves — and it won't be long before we are striking up relationships with inanimate objects (like Wilson the volleyball) to escape the monotony.

When you love yourself unconditionally, greed evaporates in the fullness of being. Then your attachment to money and the material changes completely. Ironically, when that happens, you attract everything in absolute abundance. Yet your focus is no longer on acquiring things; your focus is on love. Letting go of greed doesn't necessarily mean letting go of possessions, but maybe you'll find that you don't want as much as you thought you did. Maybe you'll just want things to be simpler.

Sloth

Sloth, or laziness, is a lack of passion for life. It is careless and disinterested, preferring comfort over achievement, stagnation over evolution. Laziness stems from self-protection, fear of risk. Love is never lazy. Love is an endless source of energy, delighting in giving and creating. Laziness takes; love gives. Laziness is heavy; love is light. Laziness begets laziness: the more you feed it, the more it wants. So start pushing the limits: get out of bed and go for a jog! If you want to feel different, do something different.

Wrath

Wrath is a distorted expression of anger. Anger is a natural human response, but we have come to judge it as evil or wrong. As a result, many of us try to suppress it, but then it only builds up inside until finally it bursts. The best way to heal wrathful impulses in ourselves and in the world is to embrace our anger; beating on a pillow or screaming into one is a healthy way of releasing anger's accumulated charge.

Another of my favorite Bible quotations is "Let not the sun go down on your wrath" (Ephesians 4:26). If we express our anger and let it transform into love on any given day rather than suppressing it and going to bed angry, we will always embrace the new day from a place of joy and optimism.

Wrath begets wrath. The character of Dexter, from the popular TV series of the same name, exemplifies this principle. He became a serial killer to escape the trauma of his own violent past. Instead of going deeper and healing what was underneath, he became addicted to the sin that caused his initial hurt. Similarly, many sex offenders have suffered abuse in their own lives. If we allow rage and hatred to build up within us, it only creates more of the same, and we often come to harbor aspects of that same behavior in ourselves.

Envy

Envy means wanting what you don't have, comparing yourself to others, casting yourself as a victim, as less than someone else. It is the opposite of embracing yourself in your own unique perfection. The cure for envy is love of self. Instead of coveting your neighbor's wife, find the pleasure of what life has brought before you. Embrace your reality instead of constantly comparing it with one you perceive as better, and celebrate the greatness of who you are: the unique brilliance that only you can bring to the world.

Pride

We invest a huge amount of energy in how we are seen by the world. Pride is this presentation; it is the false "I" we present to those around us. When we are proud, we close the door on vulnerability and innocence; we're too concerned with putting forth an image to the world to allow our real selves to shine through. As it says in the Bible, "pride comes before a fall"; because pride is fragile, dependent on external opinion, it leads to disappointment. It causes us to cling to who we think we are instead of connecting with our true selves. Pride comes from identifying so much with our personal history that we start to believe the story we have created about ourselves. In the Charles Dickens novel *Bleak House*, Lady Dedlock prefers to die rather than to remove the mask of good standing she has put on herself, in defense of her pride and that of her husband. Many real people fall into the same trap. Pride makes us rigid, because we must conform to the standard we have set for ourselves. It shuts us out to the possibility of expanding our horizons and opening to new ideas. It stops us from embracing the frailties of our human experience, for fear of losing control.

Pride causes people to commit atrocities. In times gone by, how many families disinherited their beloved children out of pride, because the children had chosen inappropriate partners, from a different religion or social class? How many gauntlets have been thrown down and lives lost in the defense of pride?

One of the best ways to break through pride is to allow yourself to look ridiculous. Don't take yourself so seriously! Let yourself look vulnerable in front of others, and see how it makes you feel. In doing so, you will be sharing yourself more with those around you, and you will also be getting to know yourself better.

GUILTY AS CHARGED

Have you not subconsciously acted out, or at least been tempted to act out, every one of the above behaviors at some point in your life? The funny thing is that these so-called sins actually do take you to hell — your own personal hell, here on Earth, because you feel so guilty about them that you lose the present moment; you lose the love and the capacity to give, locked as you are in your guilt.

Guilt is the glue that keeps us stuck in the past, bound to the very decisions we regret so much. We torture ourselves until life becomes a vicious cycle of the same repetitive behaviors.

Guilt is a form of self-flagellation — it harms nobody but ourselves. Giving is the antidote to guilt. It gets us out of our introverted obsession with what is wrong with us.

Nothing can be gained by harboring guilt. Instead of wallowing in regret, use the wisdom you have earned from your past experiences to make new choices in this moment, to re-define who you wish to be now.

What do I choose in this moment?

Don't judge yourself for your unconscious behaviors. Be the forgiveness of the Father, for you knew not what you did. Choose to be conscious now. Realize that ultimately there was never anything to forgive…for you never did anything wrong.

FREEDOM FROM ADDICTION

These seven aspects of unconscious behavior are the manifestations of separation from self, and they lead to addictive behavior. When we think of the word *addiction*, we usually think of drugs or alcoholism. Many of us may think we are not addicted to anything, yet modern society in general is full of addictive behaviors. Anything we use to distract ourselves is a form of addiction. In fact, all addictions stem from the need to get away from what we are feeling, to numb the pain, the emptiness, the disillusionment. Maybe we use the television or the internet to get away from ourselves. Maybe we open the fridge or light a cigarette whenever we feel anxious. The form the addiction takes varies, as does the level of obsession surrounding the behavior, but all addiction is rooted in the feeling of inner discontent.

Love of self is the only way to permanently heal addictive behavior. Until you come to love yourself unconditionally, you may end one addictive behavior, but before long you'll just replace it with another one. For example, how many ex-smokers quickly gain weight because they eat compulsively to replace the smoking? Cutting away the leaves of a habit is not the solution; new foliage will grow back soon enough. If you want to be free of addiction, heal the root. Go inward and fill the emptiness with love. Then your addictions will fall away by themselves, for there will be no emptiness left for them to fill.

THE POWER OF VULNERABILITY AND SELF-LOVE

As adults, most of us don't know what it means to love ourselves. "You need to love yourself," has become a catchphrase, a clever comment to throw around at dinner parties, but aside from conveying a vague idea of self-confidence, it remains an abstract concept. Many of the most confident-looking people in the world do not love themselves at all. I know; I was one of them. To the world around me, I always appeared outgoing, entertaining, and charming, but these qualities were merely a mask that hid my insecurities from view.

Self-love starts with self-acceptance. In order to love yourself, you must embrace the parts of yourself that you reject. Resentment, jealousy, anger, shame — it is by loving these parts of yourself that you will become free of them. True strength will come only when you discover the power of vulnerability: the indispensable quality that forges fluent and transparent communication in all our human relationships.

Vulnerability is something most of us avoid at all costs. It is the last position we would want to be in, and certainly not something we would actively seek! Society tells us that to be vulnerable is to be weak, but quite the opposite is true. Great power can be found in vulnerability, the power of truth. When we are vulnerable, we are being real. We are showing ourselves exactly as we are. Vulnerability allows us to embrace what is, and in that acceptance we can become more love and heal ourselves with the strength of our being.

Couples often visit my retreat center in Uruguay, sometimes on the brink of divorce. They have usually been hiding secrets from each other, not expressing how they feel, compromising themselves in order to please. In many cases, they have been unfaithful. All of this has created so much resentment that the love seems completely absent from what was previously a fulfilling, mutually loving relationship. Then they start to express all their judgments, to take the skeletons out of the closet — all the little infidelities, lies, and deceptions. The interesting thing is that after the initial shock and the realization that both partners are experiencing the same disillusionment, the love that was present when they first met starts to reemerge. This is the magic of vulnerability. You cannot fully understand it until you try it for yourself.

Vulnerability and emotion constitute the language of the heart. When I am vulnerable, my heart is open to give and to receive. It is not guarded by the falsity of masks or deception. When you dare to be vulnerable, you step outside your comfort zone, into the unknown. You let go of control, you confront the fear of rejection, and you put your own truth above the need to please others. Vulnerability is the ultimate act of self-love, the key to breaking free of codependency and releasing the flimsy crutch of external approval. Try it. Maybe you will discover the unique beauty that lies in the parts of yourself you have learned to avoid.

When I first began to allow myself to be vulnerable, I was shocked by what I found. I had always been a very strong woman, with everything under control, so I was amazed to find a little girl within me: needy, abandoned, afraid, disillusioned, and insecure. I came to love her exactly as she was, and only then could my greatness finally emerge. This is true for all of us.

We need to love that inner child who hides behind the masks of personality in order to protect her fragility. In the light of love she will transform into more love, as everything does in the embrace of acceptance. Don't be afraid of feeling and releasing what you have hidden or denied. It requires much more effort to ignore the inner aspects calling for attention than it does to give the unconditional love that they require.

If you reject or push away some aspect of yourself, it only gets bigger. You have to embrace it — it is a part of you and you cannot deny it forever. Don't label it as something bad or wrong; embrace it with honesty and acceptance.

One of the things I most judged in myself was my fear of abandonment. It was present in all my relationships, the enduring legacy of my childhood adoption. I used to mask it by feigning indifference, but beneath my apparent nonchalance, I secretly did everything possible to keep my fear from becoming a reality. I hid this behavior from my partners, terrified that if they saw my neediness I would appear fragile and unattractive. I myself judged neediness in others as weak and undesirable, and felt disdain toward people who displayed these qualities.

I repeated this dynamic many times in my life, until I found myself breaking up from one last relationship, in which the fear of loss and abandonment had reached such an extreme I could bear it no longer. I finally understood that my security could not be based in the external, that I had to cultivate an internal experience of love-consciousness and find stability within myself.

So ultimately my suffering brought me to transform these aspects into a new perception of life. When I was sick and tired of suffering, I finally made a new choice.

When I finally embraced the needy part of myself I was able to accept neediness in those around me. By embracing our own humanity, we can find the beauty in every aspect of human expression.

When I found the courage to see all of myself, without ignoring or denying any aspect, I saw that there was nothing wrong. I befriended my jealousy, my violence, my capacity to do many fear-based things, things I had previously judged harshly in others. When I embraced everything I had previously suppressed, what happened?

It all transformed into love, for it had always been love, only I had been afraid; I had wanted someone else to take responsibility for loving me, instead of doing it myself.

The extremes of our self-rejection are played out on the world stage. In some, the self-rejection is so great that it drives them to violence. Yet if we learn to embrace every aspect of ourselves, our suffering and our capacity for violence dissolve in the frequency of love. Say yes to your inner being. Love yourself, embrace yourself in unconditional love, and the world will do the same.

Over recent years, the work of my foundation has brought me to several prisons throughout Latin America. One of the things that has affected me the most during these visits is the sincere desire for transformation that I see in so many of the inmates. I have heard prisoners say that they now realize they were never free, even before prison life; they are beginning to discover an internal freedom that no walls can contain.

One particular story stands out clearly in my memory. A prisoner involved in our programs told us that no one had come to visit him in the fifteen years he had been in jail. He had felt abandoned and rejected, a forgotten outcast, and for years had harbored silent resentment toward his friends and family. He came to blame them and their indifference for his low self-worth and dejection.

By following the guidelines our program set out for him, he began to go inward. He started taking responsibility for his own inner state and came to realize that he was feeling resentful and disheartened not because his loved ones didn't visit but because he didn't love himself. This was a tremendous realization for him, to finally stop blaming the outside and start taking responsibility for his own inner change. If he can do that, in prison, what is stopping you from doing the same?

Contemplation

- Have you been acting out any of the fear-based behaviors known as the seven deadly sins? Which ones are you most prone to?
- Have you been carrying around guilt as a result?
- Where do you avoid being real in your personal relationships? Often we have the most difficulty being honest with those we are closest to. Observe the places where you hide, where you steer clear of moments of intimacy and emotion. Try doing the opposite of what you would normally do: try challenging the limits you have put on yourself. You will begin to discover new facets of life, places of magic and discovery.

CHAPTER EIGHT

Illusion #8: I Can and Should Control My World

EXPRESSED IN THE BELIEF: *If I try hard enough, I can take control of my world, and this is a good thing!*

REALITY: *Love-consciousness means surrendering to what is.*

We live in a world that is constantly changing. Recent natural disasters have made these changes ever more evident, an intense reminder of the unpredictability of our surroundings. One recent disaster that hit close to home for me was the 2010 earthquake in Chile. The lives of many of my friends and students were affected by the quake. A group of Chileans was left stranded at my center in Uruguay, unable to return home until flights to Santiago resumed. They couldn't even communicate with their families. It was as though the entire country had the phone off the hook for long, long hours.

When faced with catastrophe, a profound sense of vulnerability leaves us feeling exposed and at a loss for answers. Shocked by the horror of the explicit images in the media, we are reminded once again of how transitory everything is in life, of the futility of the race for material gain, which provides only an illusion of security, a security that can disappear in a moment. It reminds us that we cannot control even the most significant and fundamental thing in our lives: the ground beneath our feet. We are enveloped in the most extreme feeling of fragility.

In these situations of disaster and devastation, we hear stories about the blossoming of countless anonymous heroes, heroes moved by love into ceaseless giving, even to the point of risking their own safety; heroes who, beyond gender, class, or creed, go out to the streets and give. Roused by the force of love, they simply share, consoling the lost and wounded, embracing the panicked and the bereaved.

In moments like these, we forget our past disputes and conflicts. The only thing that is real is the love we feel for one another, uniting us in limitless action. In these selfless actions we can see that the consciousness of humanity is rising, with support arriving ever faster in response to these extreme situations. We see how love prevails over pain and fear. It is always present, with myriad faces and expressions, but in essence, it is always love.

When the outside becomes unstable, if our focus turns inward we can recognize that our differences don't matter, that within each of us vibrates a *yes* to life, a *yes* to moving forward, a *yes* to going beyond that which has fallen away. Even if we feel lost, we can all bring our attention into our hearts — feel them beat, feel their warmth. Within them we can discover love-consciousness. It is inexhaustible, unlimited; the more it gives, the more it has to share. This is the time — this is the shared embrace. Although we cannot understand why these disasters happen, and although we feel afraid, we can find comfort by remembering that within us all lies an unchanging place of peace and that the love will never leave.

It's time for us all to transform ourselves through the actions of love. Then we will come to realize that everything that happens is for evolution. Let's learn to dance in the face of devastation, in the face of difficulties, in the face of whatever life brings us. Even more important, let's learn to see through the illusion of control, to realize that in reality life has no guarantees, to embrace the unpredictable nature of existence instead of trying in vain to tame the untamable power of the world.

GOING WITH THE FLOW

I was flying my hawk yesterday. Watching her swoop down in the evening half-light is like a dream.

Sat is a Harris hawk, majestic and strong. Because I lovingly raised and trained her, she knows to come when I call; I am her source of food and protection. I let her go, then I whistle for her to return. Yesterday, as she was about to take off on her journey back to my glove, a strong wind came up between us. She was hungry, so she wanted to fly to the glove, but the wind was very strong. I watched as Sat took off into the air, her focus never straying from the glove. The wind took her right off in the opposite direction, but to my surprise, she didn't fight against it. She just went with the wind. She never lost sight of her goal, but she wasn't attached to how she was going to get there. She was willing to flow. She soared majestically with the current, riding the ever-shifting breeze.

She waited calmly for the wind to change, and when it did, she returned to me and claimed her prize.

This scene struck me as a perfect illustration of the wisdom of nature. Nature flows. As humans, we have lost this ability. We cling to the idea of what we want, and fight against the current of life, because our ideas are so rigid that we're not open to letting them go. No wonder we're not always in a state of joy, of peace; we're fighting against our present reality.

We all have wings, but if we fight against the wind we cannot fly. We can't experience the full magnitude of who we are. We all have unlimited potential, but when we try to control, clinging to our ideas of how we want things to be, we can't experience life in its fullness.

When we start to base our security and well-being on our inner state, our reliance on the shifting sands of the external begins to diminish. The need to control falls away. This is true freedom, for if we depend upon that which we cannot control and which constantly changes (the external), then how can we ever feel free? We are slaves of the things and people around us, as long as our stability depends on them. But if we learn to cultivate inner fulfillment, we can enjoy the world we live in without the fear of loss or the need to control it. This allows us to finally let go of our constant need to worry and plan.

Life is an experience. That's all it is. Embrace your human experience, in all its colors, in all its complexities, in its ever-changing currents. The more you flow, the more you choose the joy that is present in every moment, the greater your creative power will be. Choose love, and you will find the true majesty of yourself.

How to Surrender to Sleep

A very common result of excessively trying to control is insomnia. Insomnia is caused by our inability to switch off. We spend so much time worrying and trying to control the world around us that it becomes impossible for us to stop. You have surely noticed this when on vacations: you can be on a beach in paradise, or witnessing a breathtaking panoramic view from a mountain peak, and yet the mind continues to churn. It is impossible for us to switch off, to just be, to fully savor life as it is right now.

We have become so accustomed to planning, worrying, organizing, controlling that we have forgotten how to step back and exist in the moment. When we go to bed at night, we find that the mind continues. The body wants to rest, but the intellect is out of control, racing ahead of itself, lost in a permanent state of distraction and concern.

Just as we have developed the habit of constant distraction, we can develop a new habit: the habit of being present, of focusing on the beauty of this moment. At first, it seems difficult, but this is only because we have spent so long doing the opposite. If we start to make a habit of bringing our awareness into this moment, the results soon begin to show. If we learn to bring ourselves into the present moment when we lie down at the end of the day, we just might find that sleep comes without a struggle.

Sleep is a time when we are alone with ourselves. Let's learn to savor our own company, instead of avoiding looking inward at all costs. This will make sleep more enjoyable, and certainly easier to attain.

It is important to not get attached to the idea of sleeping. If we become obsessed with the thought that we need to sleep, it can make us agitated and push sleep farther from us. The idea that things should be a certain way, different from how they are, is what stops us from relaxing into this moment, embracing the situation. If we cannot do that, we surely will not be able to surrender to the arms of sleep.

In recent years, I've had the pleasure of working with one of the most legendary actresses of South America. Virtually everyone knows her beauty and talent, yet not so many know that she has suffered from severe insomnia since the age of thirteen. At first, although she is a deeply spiritual woman, she was somewhat dubious that something as simple as the Isha System could in any way change her life. But, much to her surprise, it solved the insomnia that had affected her entire adult life. She later told me that before learning the system she would often start her days crying from lack of sleep. Now she can face her daily work with a newfound joy, thanks to the restorative power of something we so often take for granted: a good night's rest.

It has been phenomenal to see how quickly people heal insomnia by practicing the facets I teach. The facets are designed to anchor our awareness in the present moment, and make a habit out of it, instead of just something we remember to do every now and then. I call this the "stabilization of consciousness": when our awareness is anchored permanently in the peace and stability that lie within, irrespective of what might be occurring in our surroundings.

LOSING CONTROL

There was once a great river who from her humble begin-nings as a mountain brook dreamed of reaching the ocean. She passed through forests and canyons on her journey, through plains and ravines, until one day she arrived at the desert. Just as she had moved through all other ob-stacles, the river tried to move through the desert, but she was dismayed to find that her waters dissolved as they touched the baking sand.

The river was convinced, however, that her destiny was to reach the ocean, and so she tried with all her might to cross the sands. Yet it was an impossible task — no matter how hard she tried, the river could not beat the desert.

When finally she had given up all hope, a voice whispered from the desert itself, "Just as the wind crosses the desert, so may the river."

The river objected, complaining that her waters were absorbed by the sand no matter how hard she tried, that the wind was able to cross because it could fly.

"Violently slamming yourself against me will not help you cross," the desert told her. "You will disappear completely, or at least become a swamp. You must allow the wind to take you to your destination. You must be ab-sorbed by the wind."

This idea was unacceptable to the river. After all, she had never been absorbed before. She didn't want to lose her individuality. If she did, would she ever get it back?

"The wind," said the voice, "will perform that function too. It will carry your water across the desert, and then let it fall. Falling as rain, your water will become a river once more."

"How do I know that is true?"

"It just is, and if you don't trust it, you are destined to become a swamp…and a swamp is certainly not the same as a river."

"But can't I continue being the same river I am now?"

"You cannot remain as you are under any circumstances," the voice continued. "Your essence will be transported and will form a river again. You call yourself 'river' because you do not know your essence."

As the river heard this, a distant echo began to call from beyond her thoughts. She vaguely remembered a state in which she, or a part of her — which part could it have been? — had been carried in the arms of the wind. She also remembered — or was she just imagining? — that this was really what she was meant to do, even though it didn't seem that way.

When you give up your individuality, you become the totality.

So it was that the river gave her waters up to the welcoming arms of the wind, which gently lifted her high into the sky, whisking her far away, before finally letting her fall, as rain, to the sea.

Contemplation

In what areas of your life do you excessively try to control things?

- Do you habitually try to control your partner? The need to control comes from fear, not love. If you truly love your partner, let them be. Pay more attention to yourself, and learn to love the ways in which your partner does their own thing rather than behaving exactly as you would.

- Do you attempt to micromanage your schedule and then get stressed-out when circumstances don't cooperate and you have more or less time than you'd expected? Organization is a good thing — I myself am a highly organized person — but recognize the things you cannot change, and don't get agitated when they don't go your way. Efficiency comes from being able to flow, not from rigidly bashing your head against a wall that refuses to budge.

- Do you set goals for yourself and then concoct elaborate expectations of how you want things to turn out? Expectations are basically conditions we put upon the world, rigid ideas of *how things should be*. Then, when things don't go as we expected, we experience disappointment and frustration. Let go of your expectations and work toward your goals, inwardly surrendered to what is.

CHAPTER NINE

Illusion #9: It's Okay to Ignore Unpleasant Feelings

EXPRESSED IN THE BELIEF: *If I ignore the things I don't like, they will go away.*

REALITY: *In order to evolve I have to confront my emotions and embrace my fears.*

During my recent trip to the Netherlands, I was fascinated to learn how Dutch engineers had employed remarkable techniques to reclaim massive areas from the sea. The country itself is a triumph of human ingenuity.

Surprisingly, some of the dikes that hold back the water are built from sand. One would imagine they would all be built from steel and concrete in order to resist the force of the ocean, but the engineers understood that the sea was too powerful to fight against, so instead of trying to block it out, they allowed it to seep through the dikes. I was amazed to learn that as the water filters through the dikes, the salt is removed, and on the other side the water is fresh.

This struck me as a wonderful analogy for the process of healing. If we resist our fears and accumulated emotions, their force can destroy us: the pressure builds up until it can be held back no more and explodes in rage, violence, or despair, or even manifests as physical sickness. Yet if we allow our emotions to flow through us, they become sweet; as the salt water is purified, so our accumulated emotions flow into a river of love. It is by embracing and accepting, flowing with the forces within us that we find harmony.

DO YOU AVOID YOUR EMOTIONS?

Emotions are a natural part of human life. If we are working toward a healthy relationship with ourselves, it is essential that we learn to embrace them. Most of us learn from an early age that certain emotions are "bad" or inappropriate — for example, maybe we were told not to cry, or never to get angry.

By denying these feelings, we don't rid ourselves of them. When an emotion is ignored, it stagnates within us, building up and contributing to the accumulated charge of repressed feelings. With time, these emotions become distorted: anger becomes hatred or resentment, eventually exploding in fits of rage and violence; sadness becomes depression.

We need only to look at a child to see how natural emotions are. Children get angry and sad with spontaneous ease, yet they have an innate ability to find joy and entertainment everywhere. The world for them is a magical place, and where we adults would find only boredom, they are capable of discovering wonderment. This is precisely because they don't deny any aspect of their emotional spectrum. Without judgment they embrace all its hues as natural parts of the human experience. As a result, when anger comes, it is intense but short-lived. Five minutes later, they have completely forgotten what they were angry about, absorbed in the excitement of a new moment, the next discovery.

Sometimes, when we are on the spiritual path, we apply the same "shoulds" and "shouldn'ts" of our childhood conditioning to our process of growth; we try to box ourselves into an image of the "good" boy or girl — an image that is not so far removed from the expectations placed on us by our parents and our society. The quest for unconditional love becomes a way of behaving: we try to emulate the actions of love and compassion without first becoming those experiences. This eventually leads to more resentment and frustration, for how can you embrace another in their perfection if you still see yourself as imperfect? How can you be compassionate toward others if you do not love yourself? In trying to break free from the confines of our past limitations, we jump into a new box, sometimes even more rigid than the one before.

In order to experience our divinity, we must first embrace our humanity. In order to love unconditionally, we must first discover our own perfection. Embrace your anger, embrace your sadness. It is not through denial that you will be free of them, but through acceptance. By allowing yourself to feel the accumulated charge of your emotions, you free up space within yourself. Space to be, space to love, space to discover who you truly are.

No Hard Feelings: Letting Go of Resentment

Resentment builds up when we are not real with the people in our lives. What we leave unsaid causes resentment, often little things that pile on top of each other, until the tiniest event can cause an explosive reaction. Try incorporating the following habits into your life to free yourself from resentment.

Say What You Feel, in the Moment

Speaking our truth is one of the hardest things for us to do, and telling people — especially the people we love and admire — when we are annoyed with them is often extremely difficult. The reason it is so hard is that we are afraid of rejection, of losing their approval and ultimately their love. Yet when we don't say what we are feeling, we store inside ourselves the momentary irritation or conflict that their actions generated, adding it to the collection of similar annoyances we have repressed over the course of the relationship. These emotions become an energetic barrier that impedes the love we feel from flowing freely. Every time we see the person, we are subconsciously reminded of those moments that bothered us, and so, instead of being fully present in embracing the person as they are, afresh in each moment, we are distracted, focusing on what is wrong. The spontaneity of the relationship is then gone.

If we pretend to be nice and friendly, our interactions become a performance — an act, where true love is hard to find. On the other hand, when we decide to face the fear of rejection and say what we are really feeling, something incredible happens. Our transparency sets us free, allowing us to release the judgments and emotions we have built up over time, and let go of resentment. We can then return to the appreciation and innocence that the relationship once had.

So many couples grow apart over time because of this pattern: out of fear of losing each other, they hide what they really feel. The result? Two people who are physically close but distanced inside.

Develop a Loving Relationship with Yourself

For most of our lives, in order to be accepted and loved we compromise, abandoning ourselves to do what other people want — what our parents want, what our spouses want, what society wants. Now we can make a new choice, a higher choice to start loving ourselves unconditionally and accepting ourselves exactly as we are.

The need to receive approval from our loved ones, the need to control and manipulate their opinion of us, comes from our need for acceptance and love. It is only when we have lost the ability to accept ourselves that we start worrying about what other people think, and so start hiding and contorting ourselves in order to become what we consider "good enough." In order to change this, we must go inward and look honestly at ourselves.

Start listening to yourself. Worry less about how the outside tells you to be and start listening to the voice of your own heart. This will make it easier for you to speak your truth and let go of the need for external approval.

Feel Your Emotions

In order to release the built-up charge of resentment, allow yourself to feel. Let yourself get angry; permit yourself to feel sad. When you do, you will find that the resentment and bitterness from events of the past begin to lift, and you are able to recuperate the magic and innocent wonder of childhood.

Overcoming Shyness

When shyness overshadows our talents, we miss out on opportunities to grow and advance. We become trapped in a vicious cycle of insecurity and frustration.

Shyness is often masked as disinterest or indifference, yet its root is much deeper. If we go deep into the feeling of shyness, we will discover pure fear — fear of what others might think of us, fear of disapproval.

In order to be free of shyness, the only thing we need to do is find security within ourselves — to reach the point where what we think of ourselves becomes more important than any external opinion. Shyness is fed by thoughts of self-criticism. Often these thoughts have been instilled in us by a judgmental or authoritarian figure in our past who made us feel like less than we were. Sometimes a specific traumatic or shocking event in our past has left its mark, paralyzing our natural expression and replacing it with the fear of standing out and an internal feeling of inadequacy. Irrespective of the origin, what matters is that when our shyness is activated, instead of acting out the same old defensive reactions, we listen to our hearts and dive deeper, beyond the fear, allowing our natural talents to shine through.

During the time of my life when I first started singing professionally, I faced any kind of challenge with alcohol. I was incredibly shy, and I drank in order to drown out my insecurity. I was terrified of what people might think of me, and drinking made me feel brave. The only thing I couldn't do drunk was sing, because I couldn't get the notes right. So the first time I went onstage sober, I was shaking. I was so afraid that I stood behind the guitarist! The first song I sang was "I

Fall to Pieces" by Patsy Cline, and no other phrase could have better described my emotional state in that moment. I was indeed falling to pieces, and of course all my friends had come to listen — which only made matters worse — but I got through it. I don't know if I sang well, but the important thing was that I did it. That is how you move beyond fear — by just doing it.

If you feel daunted by a new project, don't waste time worrying. If you are afraid of letting go of the known and trying something different, as you walk toward the new choice, let go of the old; when the fear comes, continue forward, feeding the enthusiasm of the heart, not the doubts of the mind.

Your stomach shrinks, you feel insecure, but if you keep bringing yourself into the moment, as your feet continue ahead, your fear will be eclipsed by the excitement of the heart.

There are no guarantees for cultivating trust in yourself. You trust by trusting, by walking through your fears and letting go of your protection and control. You trust by choosing once and again to embrace life instead of resisting, and in doing so, realizing that the best is always coming to you, even though it may not seem that way.

Once you dwell in love-consciousness, there is nothing you cannot do, because you feel secure within yourself. That sense of security is the most important thing you can give to yourself — because you deserve love, you deserve to shine.

ARE YOU ATTACHED TO YOUR IMAGE?

As adults, we are terrified of losing approval. We pretend all the time in order to be accepted by others, creating a false image that we present to the world, hiding our true feelings.

When we do this, we are abandoning ourselves. Other people's approval is a weak and unstable substitute for self-love. It will never be enough to fully satisfy us, for if we have to modify ourselves in order to be loved, how can we ever feel comfortable in our own skin?

On the journey back to love of self, showing yourself as you really are and speaking the truth are essential. This is scary at first: as we start to expose the parts of ourselves we have learned to judge, the fear of rejection is unavoidable.

Yet speaking the truth is like a muscle; it's the muscle of the heart. The more you use that muscle, the stronger it will grow. The truth becomes an energy that moves outward; it is the energy of the heart.

Be yourself, and love your uniqueness completely.

An image is a copy of something else, a fabricated idea. No false image could ever live up to the unique luminosity of your internal diamond. Be yourself, and love your uniqueness completely. Then you will finally feel approved of, because you will be approving of yourself.

EMBRACING YOUR FEARS

When we finally decide to confront the aspects of ourselves we have learned to ignore, it is natural to experience fear. It's scary to face the things we have come to judge about ourselves. So how do we overcome this fear? By walking toward it. When you walk toward fear, it disappears...

Once upon a time, there was a man who decided to go to a self-help workshop on his thirtieth birthday. The facilitators told him that he needed to confront his fears. On his way home, he racked his brain to think of his biggest fear so that he could confront it. Suddenly he remembered the old house on the edge of town. Everyone knew it was haunted, and ever since he was a child he had been terrified of it. He had heard such awful stories of what went on inside that he was afraid of even going past it and habitually took the long way back from work just to avoid the house.

After much thought, he decided that this was his biggest fear, and that in order to confront it, he would have to spend a night there.

Everyone thought he was crazy, but he was determined to complete the workshop's assignment. He packed a flashlight and sleeping bag into his knapsack and set off down the road, as clouds covered the moon, leaving him walking alone through the black, starless night.

As he reached the huge iron gates, his heart began beating faster, but he was determined. He pushed open the creaking gates, walked through them, and made his way down the path leading to the yawning black chasm of the shadowy doorway. He jumped in fright as the gates slammed shut behind him, but he continued on his way. The house was huge and ominous in the dark, its old shutters hiding its contents from view.

As he walked into the gloomy hallway, a wind started to whistle through the corridors, whisking a heavy dust into the air and shaking the cobwebs that hung from every corner.

Making his way up the creaking staircase, he stopped more than once, convinced that one of the shriveled old faces of the many hanging portraits had turned to glare at him with distaste. Pulling himself together, he continued his journey, up into the attic. He was determined to look his fear right in the face, and although he was shivering all over, nothing was going to stop him.

Fear is just love with an ugly face.

When he finally reached the small attic room at the top of the winding stair, he set out his sleeping bag and settled down for the night.

This isn't so bad after all, *he thought, drifting off into a warm, deep sleep.*

Suddenly, he was jerked awake by a huge crashing sound. Frightened and disoriented, he jumped up and listened at the door. His heart almost stopped when he heard the heavy footsteps — boom, boom — making their way up the stairs.

As he started to imagine what sort of terrible beast he was about to behold, a strangled wailing sound floated up from the stairwell, accompanied by a rattling of chains.

Shaking with terror and realizing there was no way out, he heard the monster climb straight up to the room where he was cowering.

Just as the monster was about to reach the door of the room, he made a decision and told himself, I don't care how horrible the monster is; whatever comes through that door, I am going to give it a great big hug!

In that moment, he woke up. Warm morning light was pouring through the old shutters.

There had been no monster; it was just a dream!

When you dare to embrace the monsters that haunt you, they disappear.

Contemplation

- Is there a particular relationship in your life in which you have been repressing your feelings instead of speaking your mind? If so, consider having a heart-to-heart talk with that person to let them know what has been bothering you. Speak from a place of compassion and love, and be open to hear what they have to say in response. Afterward, notice how you feel and how the relationship feels. Chances are, either the relationship will feel stronger and more loving or you'll know it's time to move on. Either way, you're likely to feel a tremendous sense of relief from having aired your repressed emotions.

- In what situations do you step back instead of stepping up? Make a list of those situations. Just by writing them down, you will become more honest with yourself about what you want to achieve, and you'll be more likely to step into your greatness. Every time you feel you are putting the brakes on yourself, take another step forward. Don't worry about the consequences — just keep moving forward, releasing the brakes bit by bit, and soon things will flow more naturally.

PART TWO

*Infusing Your Roles
and Responsibilities
with Love-Consciousness*

At the age of twenty-eight, I lost everything. I lost my money, my property, my social standing, my boyfriend, my grandmother who had raised me with my parents, and my father; plus my mother had a stroke. Everything that gave me external security was completely eradicated from my life within a six-month period.

This time of loss left the image of who I thought I was lying in pieces. The roles I had identified with for so long no longer existed, and with them went my sense of self.

Now, many years later, I look back on who I used to be and feel like a totally different person. The transformations I went through around that time were what eventually brought me to South America, and my life has become something I would never have dreamed of.

Losing all that was familiar gave me the freedom to re-invent myself unfettered by the ideas I had about who I was supposed to be. This is why loss can be such a great teacher, for in loss we are faced with our own feelings of emptiness. Suddenly unable to distract ourselves with our addictions or delusions of choice, we become aware of the hole inside us — now open and visible, impossible to ignore any longer. We then have two choices: we can try to hide it again — by rebuilding that which we have lost, recasting ourselves in stereotypical roles, and/or resorting to the same or new forms of distraction; or we can finally decide to take responsibility for our feeling of inadequacy and begin to do the necessary work to find completion within.

But it doesn't take personal tragedy or loss to enable us to do that. We can decide to make changes right here, right now — after all, even if we are not experiencing tumultuous change in our personal lives, we can certainly see that things are changing rapidly in the world at large. Decades ago, fears disguised as prejudices formed ideologies of all kinds that controlled the way we behaved as human beings, telling us how to be, with blatant disregard for the feelings and desires of the individual. At this point in the evolution of humanity, long-held, rigid ideas about gender, career, and familial roles are being replaced with a feeling of "anything goes" — men are staying home to keep house and care for the kids, women are rising to positions of power in business and government, men are undergoing surgical procedures to become women and vice versa, and parents are empowering their children to make adult decisions rather than dictating how their children should act and inflicting harsh punishments when they diverge from the preconceived notions of appropriate behavior. As never before in history, we are empowered to examine the labels we put on ourselves and how we perform the corresponding roles, rather than blindly following established norms.

The following incident, which took place when I first established a retreat center in Colombia, shows just how illusory the labels we put on ourselves and others really are.

As I was driven through the jungle, I asked the driver the name of the head of the paramilitary. I was on my way to visit him, having recently arrived in what turned out to be his territory. The oceanfront hilltop where we had built our center was in the middle of a so-called red zone, "protected" by the paramilitaries who looked over us like the Sierra Nevada de Santa Marta, the tallest coastal mountain range in the world.

It turned out that his name was Jesus. I thought to myself ironically, *Let's hope Jesus is my friend.*

Jesus was. He was charming, delighted that I was teaching a form of expansion of consciousness so close to his beloved city. He assured me that if I had any trouble, he would swiftly deal with anyone who was impeding my stay. I avoided asking exactly how he was planning on dealing with them, opting instead to just smile sweetly.

Here I was, a spiritual teacher in the middle of the jungle, proposing union in a province where paramilitaries and guerrilla soldiers shared only their dislike of the government.

One morning, the sound of heavy footsteps drowned out the rhythmic rumble of the ocean that usually coaxed us out of bed, as a troop of heavily armed soldiers clomped purposefully up the steps. Dressed in black, laden with grenades and guns that would require a heavy workout just to be carried, they assembled sternly on our veranda. With the spectacular tropical panorama framing them, they looked like intruders on someone's vacation.

They were antinarcotic police under President Uribe's command, but we didn't know that until they presented themselves. After a few gruff questions about our intentions in the area, they put down their Uzis, hand grenades, and Rambo bullet belts, and sat to hear a brief introduction to the work of our foundation.

As they listened to us talk about love-consciousness, unconditional love, and the union that exists beyond our apparent differences, their faces displayed sincere interest and curiosity. But the most telling thing was their responses to the question, "What do you want?"

It doesn't matter where I go in the world. Whether I am speaking at a high-security prison or an international forum; to senators, catholic nuns, or ex–guerrilla soldiers — everyone has the same answers.

"Peace," said one of the soldiers. "Love," murmured another.

Peace.

Beyond our apparent differences lies the common core of consciousness, which unites us beyond all diversity. Here's an idea: why don't we focus on that instead of on the things that seem to separate us? Maybe then we would discover the peace we so yearn for.

What do you see when you see a soldier? Can you see beyond the uniform and touch on that which unites you both?

What about when you think about a man, a woman, a mother, a father, a husband, a wife, a successful professional, a boss — do you have certain assumptions about what these labels mean? The tapestry of our perception is stitched with the threads of those around us. Our mothers and fathers, schoolteachers and politicians, neighbors and religious figures all weave their colors into the fabric of our upbringing. As our perception is shaped from this web of opinions and external influences, we adopt the picture society has painted for us in lieu of being who we really are, until we finally choose to awaken to our own truth.

Now that we have explored and exposed some of the most commonly held illusions of our times, let's go deeper into our transformation. In this section of the book, we will work on breaking down the stereotypes and prefabricated roles that keep us locked in judgment and separation, that feed the fire of duality and the opinions of the mind. What do these interpersonal roles mean from the perspective of enlightenment? We have already established that love-consciousness lives without boundaries, rigid expectations, or rules; so how does it behave within these roles? We will explore some of the most common roles and how they transform in the experience of love-consciousness. We will learn to perform them not as we think we're supposed to, by enacting the stereotypes that society has beaten into our psyches through fairy tales, myths, and popular culture, but by being ourselves and infusing all our actions with compassion and love-consciousness. In so doing, we will become better men, women, mothers, fathers, lovers, life partners, employees, and entrepreneurs than we've ever been before.

CHAPTER TEN

Elevating Our Concepts of Gender

*R*ecently I watched a documentary called *Babies* that showed very clearly that infants from all cultures are born the same, displaying identical forms of expression in the first months of life. Then, bit by bit, social norms begin to modify them through the games and activities of their surroundings, and their behaviors begin to reflect that conditioning.

Surely the most fundamental type of conditioning that gets foisted on us as babies is our gender identity. From the moment we are born, people make assumptions about us based on our gender (and, since the advent of ultrasound technology, for many of us it begins even before our birth). Baby girls are dressed in pink and given dolls to play with. Baby boys are dressed in blue and handed toy trucks. This trend continues throughout childhood, and by the time we become adults we're so used to acting the way women or men are "supposed" to act that in many cases we have no idea who we would be without this gender construction.

Around masculinity and femininity, the corresponding "isms" have developed — machoism (known as machismo) and feminism — and stereotypes have been brought to such an extreme that we have even associated the sexes with different planets! Let's take this opportunity to corral some of the assumptions attached to what it means to be a man or a woman so that we can move beyond them. After all, as the *Babies* film showed, we all started out the same, and we can all embrace that common essence and become integrated beings once again.

MAN

In times gone by, a man could not be emotionally vulnerable without being discriminated against or judged. Only anger was allowed; sadness was considered a weakness. Conversely, sadness was allowed for women, yet they were not allowed to get angry. Today things are quite different, but even so, many of us have been molded by these norms.

We have learned that men must be strong and never show weakness. Often we have translated this into thinking that men must never ask for help, much to the exasperation of women everywhere, who can't convince their spouses to ask for directions when the GPS invariably sends them the wrong way. Yet the greatest casualty of the masculine stereotype is the loss of sensitivity — the place where true strength actually lies.

The male stereotype casts the man as the breadwinner and decision maker. It also instructs him to deny his emotions and even aspects of his creativity. I remember years ago arriving home exhausted after a hard day's work to find my long-term boyfriend listening carefully to my mother's cooking instructions on the phone while merrily stirring a heavily smoking frying pan. The pan was emitting smells too strange to imagine, and the kitchen was strewn with dirty pots and pans and in a state of utter chaos. As I walked through the door he announced proudly, "Meat and three veg!" as though he had personally uncovered the ultimate secret of domestic bliss and nutritional balance. My face was perplexed, as I tried to understand how he had managed to distribute his dirty clothes so evenly over every single piece of furniture and visible surface in the house. It soon became clear to me that he was living the masculine stereotype to the extreme while desperately trying (to no avail) to appear liberated!

The intense competition that modern masculinity structures itself upon only increases men's feeling of lack. It's time for a new, enlightened manhood, one that chooses cooperation over domination.

In order to return to emotional balance, men need to allow themselves to be vulnerable. When we shut down to our feelings, we also lose touch with our intrinsic wisdom. By protecting ourselves from the things we fear, we are ultimately shielding ourselves from love.

Certain protective behaviors have become the common currency of manhood, closing the doors to what men truly feel inside. A gruff rebuttal to any invitation to feel is a typical "manly" response, and anything else might be frowned upon by the typical masculine stereotype. Many aspects of the arts are considered effeminate or even "gay." So-called real men don't express pain or emotion, don't care about their appearance, and maybe even attack before they are attacked. Real men like beer, naked women, and football. They certainly don't like theater, interior design, or skin care!

I remember one of my students telling me of the ridicule and rejection he experienced as a heterosexual hairdresser in a small town in the Argentinean countryside. Even though he is married and has a child, he became accustomed to the suspicious stares and furtive gossip of his neighbors, their prejudices tainted by an outdated stereotype dictating what was expected of a "real man." My own hairdresser, on the other hand, an avant-garde stylist from the sprawling metropolis of Buenos Aires, who has been married more than once and has several children, cannot conceive of any kind of prejudice in this respect. Having grown up in a different cultural environment, a world of journalists and celebrities where he is respected, he has a self-confidence that goes beyond gender prejudice.

I grew up in a society where gender equality, racial diversity, and the acceptance of alternative sexuality were already a reality in the seventies, and upon arriving in Latin America, I found that some countries have yet to transcend prejudices that to my Australian mind seemed antiquated. Just a few days ago I read an article debating the morality of women's soccer and its effect on female sexual preferences. For many in this culture, soccer is still considered a male-only sport, and the growth of women's soccer is generating debate and disagreement.

In today's world, the only thing that really matters is that whatever we do, we do with passion and without limiting ourselves to the rigid concepts of what we think is expected of us. There have been more than enough decades of "men should..." and "men shouldn't..." already. Let's invite the men of the world to transcend stereotypical male roles and embrace their masculine and feminine aspects in their own unique expression. To enjoy their creativity in whatever form it might manifest itself, and to rejoice in their masculinity, instead of overburdening themselves with responsibility in order to prove themselves as men.

Fever Pitch

Maybe as a result of the tradition of emotional repression and competition among men, an interesting phenomenon can be observed at major sporting events. Around the world, hordes of spectators come together, and a lifetime's worth of pent-up feelings are suddenly let loose in a mass catharsis.

We cheer, we cry, we thrash about and scream, behaving in strange and unexpected ways. Sometimes the game or match is used as an excuse for violence, fed by a difference of opinion combined with masculine energy gone wild. When the game kicks off, our competitive nature reaches fever pitch, and behaviors otherwise unaccepted by society are suddenly given free rein.

For the most passionate fans among us, to support the team behind the ball, to share our enthusiasm with our companions is an enormous rush, the world watching as we celebrate our sport. But some of us get so involved that we reach the point of losing our joy, losing our happiness — we're so hell-bent on our team's winning that we forget it's a game we watch for fun.

I don't want to rain on the parade, but let's not lose sight of the true scale of things. Let's use these moments as a massive catharsis, releasing the pressure valve of our emotions; let's enjoy ourselves, maybe even observe the intensity with which we cling to the results, and learn to let go a little.

For those of us who don't express our emotions freely in our lives, this opportunity to do so does a lot of good, but those who cling to success in the results only cause themselves greater frustration, fueling their sense of "us against them" and aggressive competition.

Contemplation for Men

- In what areas of your life do you refuse to be vulnerable and sensitive, hiding your true feelings to live up to what you think is expected of you?

    Being vulnerable and sensitive will not make you weak. It will help you connect to yourself and understand more profoundly those around you. Vulnerability will allow you to communicate your needs and understand the needs of others.

- Does responsibility frighten you, leaving you feeling overwhelmed, as if the world is resting on your shoulders? Are you sustaining a false mask of control?

WOMAN

Woman, the fairer sex. Often judged as the weaker sex. The ones who should remain demure and in the background.

As a young girl, I was outspoken and confident. My strict, Victorian-style ladies' college frowned upon this behavior; it was considered unladylike. I attempted to play the part of the gentle, soft girl — to little avail — but later in life I came to realize how much of my strength and power I had abandoned in doing so. I learned to play small so that other people would feel comfortable, hiding my anger behind a mask of girlish sweetness, not staying true to my heart or trusting in my convictions.

By the age of eight, I had decided that when I grew up I would become the next Tarzan. Sadly, my conviction was soon extinguished when my mother informed me that, Tarzan or not, I could no longer run around the streets without a top on. I was indignant. What kind of lord/lady of the jungle would go around wearing a t-shirt?

"TARZAN DOESN'T WEAR A TOP!" I screamed at the top of my voice.

"Then you can't be Tarzan," my mother replied.

"But why?"

"Because girls don't wear loincloths! They wear dresses, or at least bottoms and tops."

Thus I was initiated into womanhood. From that moment on, I wore blouses and dresses and played Tarzan no more.

From the innocence of childhood, I could not conceive of a reason why I should have to be different from boys. I threw the discus and the javelin and ran track, comparing my running times with the records set by my Olympic heroes. I learned outdoor activities with my uncles in the outback, and although my grandmother tried to train me in more domestic pursuits, my real interests lay beyond the picket fence, out over the horizon in the wild expanses of the natural world. I broke in my first horse when I was only twelve years old, and from then on I never looked back, becoming one of the best in the equestrian field, a field that was dominated by men. But it was my passion that drove me, regardless of what was expected or commonplace.

Is my equestrian achievement more or less meritorious than mastering the art of weaving, cooking, or parenthood? No, it's just different. We must each listen to what our heart desires so that our actions always reflect our being, vibrating in unison with our inner drive, rather than reflecting obligation or what is expected from us.

Many beautiful qualities are typically associated with femininity: grace, emotion, creativity, the nurturing energy of motherhood. By all means, share these gifts with the world, celebrate your femininity, but don't try to box yourself into these behaviors; do what comes naturally. If your personality does not fit into a typically "feminine" mold, don't try to squeeze it in. Embrace your uniqueness and celebrate the idiosyncrasies that make you you and you alone.

Some women play dumb to make their men feel strong and important and to appear unthreatening. This is the ultimate self-abandonment and does nothing to help anyone find empowerment! How many women have stifled their power in order to make themselves small and acceptable? Our potential is unlimited, but out of self-doubt and insecurity, we have learned to avoid our greatness. How many possibilities have we left undiscovered?

Even today, in the twenty-first century, the experience of womanhood stretches between extreme polarities. On the one hand are those women who develop their potential to the limits of human achievement: the female scientists who participate in some of the greatest discoveries of our times, or those who travel to outer space on missions that were pure science fiction half a century ago. On the other hand, there are still places in the world where female genital mutilation is commonplace and even where women are stoned to death, the socially accepted punishment for those who do not respect the norms of their culture.

Between these extremes lies a rich and varied array of experiences, women of all colors and all nations, all traditions and backgrounds, adding a new chapter to the diverse and vibrant history of women in the world.

Most of us have adopted the habits of our culture, feeding the subconscious mind with fears and doubts that keep us clinging to the self-destructive patterns we have learned to emulate. Yet there are always cases of those who have risen above the hardships of their circumstances, standing as beacons of inspiration to others, their presence and achievements whispering, "Yes, you can," to the rest of us. Waris Dirie comes to mind, the Somalian former supermodel who was subjected to female circumcision and later became a voice against this ancestral practice.

We women often subject ourselves to the limiting mandates and traditions of our communities out of passivity, fear, and the need for external approval. We learn when it is easier to abandon ourselves than to stand in our power and speak our truth.

When we begin to expand our consciousness and to embrace and accept ourselves, we start to reverse this tendency. We come to realize that removing our limiting beliefs generates enthusiasm and gratitude for our surroundings, and in turn we rekindle a state of wonder within ourselves that then permeates throughout our lives.

Contemplation for Women

In what areas do you choose to be passive and abandon your power because of what you feel is expected of you as a woman?

Affirm to yourself: *As a woman I can stand in my power, be strong, and speak my truth. I don't need to abandon myself in endless giving in order to demonstrate my importance. I am important and I need to be responsible for loving myself.*

COMING BACK TO WHOLENESS

We all have a masculine and a feminine aspect. Traditionally we have tried to block out one and emphasize the other, but as collective consciousness expands, this tendency is starting to change. I can see it in the events I speak at around the world: when I first started, the audience was almost exclusively women, with the odd disgruntled husband hiding in the back row after being dragged in by his overenthusiastic wife. Now the crowd is about half and half. For me, this more universal interest in spirituality is an external indication of the internal balance that we are discovering as our consciousness rises.

Today, more and more people are finding balance. Characteristics once associated with one gender are now embraced by the other. For the new generation, unisex can describe not only clothing and hairstyles but a more androgynous presence in general. More and more people are stepping outside of the traditionally accepted roles of their gender, making choices that blur the boundaries between masculinity and femininity.

Men are integrating the emotional world, while women are integrating the world of decision making and achievement, and so feeling and doing are left in the hands of all. As time goes by, the barriers will continue to fall as the acceptance of our unique diversity reaches all points of the planet and all generations, even those stuck in ancestral ways; for in essence, we are all the same.

The more we focus on being present, the more we can shake the foundations of our subconscious fears. Then the entire structure of our mistrust and separation will crumble, and in its place, a new structure will be erected, flexible, trusting, joyful, loving, peaceful. We can embrace the present moment, no longer repressed by the limits of gender identities. Then nothing will hold us back from achieving our dreams.

CHAPTER ELEVEN

Conscious Parenting

*O*ur personalities are fundamentally influenced by our parenting. When parents instill a sense of self-worth and trust in their children, it accompanies their children throughout their adult lives. Conversely, when parents abuse their children, the resulting pain and shame the children feel will stay with them into adulthood and may lead them to abuse others.

Another expression of the power of parenting is the capacity of people raised in material abundance to always create money. They have grown up with the expectation that there will always be enough, and so that belief creates their financial reality as adults.

Unfortunately, parents throughout time have been limited by ideas about what a father or mother should and shouldn't be. By deconstructing these stereotypes and then reflecting on the legacies our parents left us with, as well as the legacies we are passing on to our kids, we can free ourselves to create a new reality for ourselves, our children, and the world.

FATHER

We have all had different experiences with our fathers. I was fortunate enough to have a father who shared his time and attention abundantly and unconditionally with me. He supported me up to the day he left this world.

Maybe your father was like mine — attentive, always looking out for what you needed. Or maybe he was the great provider, materially present but never really affectionate. Maybe you had an absent father, for whom career and social activities were the most important; maybe it is hard for you to remember a significant moment you shared with him. Maybe you don't remember any kind of affection expressed by your father.

Traditionally, the father has been boxed as a distant figure, unemotional, and removed from the lives of his children.

It used to be seen as appropriate to follow in the father's footsteps, as in, *My father was a lawyer, his father was a lawyer, and so I too will be a lawyer.* Nowadays, these expectations are falling away. The son might become a nurse while the daughter runs the farm! Stereotypes are dissolving as the line between masculinity and femininity fades into a more androgynous reality in which we embrace the masculine and feminine aspects of ourselves.

A New Vision of Fatherhood

In this new millennium fathers are emerging who are very different from the stereotypical fathers of previous centuries.

Some new beings coming into the world receive pure expressions of fatherly love from the first moments of their lives. This occurrence is a clear indication of our collective evolution in consciousness: the inner union between the structured and rational masculine aspect and the emotional and creative feminine aspect.

These new fathers, unafraid of sharing their tenderness and sensitivity, have integrated a much wider range of emotions while retaining the dynamic, practical proactivity that has traditionally been associated with masculinity. (In the same way, women are reclaiming the power and responsibility inherent in the more nourishing, warm, and gentle aspects of womanhood.) They are more connected with their own feelings, allowing them to guide their sons and daughters to greater emotional acceptance.

A conscious father leads by example, supporting his children in their greatness and instilling in them the qualities of self-acceptance, trust, and unconditional love. In order to do this, he must first develop these qualities within himself.

The more we unify within ourselves, yielding to the unconditional love that embraces all aspects of humanity, the more we will touch on the most powerful force — love-consciousness, within whose presence fear and limitations get diluted and dissolve. The result: fathers who instill love in the hearts of children who watch and imitate, loving them back unconditionally.

These children grow up being the best they can be, supported in their greatness to develop their own unique expression of self, without limiting themselves in any way in this adventure called life.

MOTHER

Our mothers influence us more than anyone else in our lives. Even in adulthood, as the years go by, their legacy lives on within us.

Some of us adore our mothers; others fight or compete with them. Some can't go a day without having a conversation with Mom; others cannot bear to even speak to her. Yet no matter what we feel, our mothers have instilled their best and worst aspects within us. Often they represent everything we love and everything we hate; we love the security and comfort they give us and hate the control they exert and fear they provoke.

When our mothers embraced and accepted us, we felt as if we could touch heaven with our bare hands; the intense emotion of maternal love, nurturing us, protecting us, and caring for us in the first days of our lives, is never erased completely. Yet the rejections, disapproval, and punishments our mothers heaped on us have also left their mark.

The formative moments we shared with our mothers are recorded so profoundly in our memories, in the hard disk that stores the information of who we think we are, that as adults we continue to project those same feelings in our personal relationships. We seek that same protection, that feeling of being nurtured and loved, and maybe even re-create the same feelings of rejection.

Because I was given up for adoption at an early age, a sense of abandonment was recorded in my hard disk. Even though my adoptive parents smothered me with love, affection, and security, I continued to feel insecure and was always anticipating the next abandonment. I would unconsciously pursue people who couldn't commit in relationships so I could re-create the feeling of not deserving or not being good enough.

Often we yearn to be as much as — or sometimes more than — our mothers. Many children with famous parents internalize the demands of success to such a point that they turn to substance abuse. They subconsciously tell themselves, *I cannot be that big, that amazing, that famous, so therefore I am not worthy*. But no matter how we look at it, our mothers are, more often than not, our greatest mirrors.

When you can honestly say that you love your mother with all your heart, without judgment or regret, you will know clearly that you are loving yourself, that you are loving the feminine aspect within. Until you reach that point, I invite you to transform what you feel toward your mother into an opportunity for self-realization.

Contemplation

How do you feel toward your mother and father? Be honest with yourself and identify what is really going on. Do you feel a need for their approval? Are you afraid of losing them? Do you resent them for all the things they left unsaid or the mistakes you think they made? Observe when you watch your words when you speak with them, and strive to be more direct and transparent in your communications. Allow yourself to feel the emotions that may have been hiding behind these protections.

When you release the stress harbored from the past, you will feel a renewed love toward your parents, whether they are physically present in your life or not. You will be able to see them afresh and to vibrate in the highest level of unconditional love you have ever felt.

Healing the World by Mothering Ourselves

I was only four years old when my mother first told me that I was adopted. The news sent me into panic, and something inside me froze.

The shock of the situation was so great that it triggered a drastic change in me. Up until that moment, I had always been a very affectionate, innocent child. Afterward, I started to avoid all physical contact. I wriggled uncomfortably whenever someone tried to embrace me; I hated being touched in any way. I decided that overtures of love could not be trusted, because the people who loved me had lied to me. I came to expect dishonesty from anyone who showed me affection, rejecting all who came too close.

In order to escape, I created fantasy worlds where I would lose myself for hours, surrounded by the vast animal kingdom of my imagination. There the animals would talk to me; they were the only ones whose love I really trusted. Devoid of all human beings, this world became my favorite place. I would run for miles into the countryside in search of my animal friends, often escaping during the night, on the quest to find another world.

Although the circumstances vary, we have all been through an initial shock of abandonment and disillusion in our lives — a situation in which we felt unloved or rejected or that in some way exposed us to loss, change, or the uncertainty of external security. It might have been a schoolteacher telling us off in front of our classmates, the loss of a loved one, a divorce, or maybe something seemingly insignificant that perhaps we don't even remember. These situations create the feeling of separation that is so integral to this human experience. Then, as we mature, we often find ourselves choosing relationships that create the same response. It is as if we are endlessly striving to prove that we really don't deserve love, that we are not good enough to receive it.

By healing the accumulated resentment and tension of our past experiences, we can unravel the misunderstandings and reproachful memories that may have left us bitter, confused, or desolate. We can heal the emotional scars left by circumstances that seemed unjust, that made us feel like victims.

If you feel undeserving, unsupported, unloved, unnoticed, or undervalued because of events from your past, the feeling represents an opportunity to move closer to unconditional love and find greater internal completion. Generally, when we don't know what to do with all these feelings, we learn to repress and ignore them. What happens then? When we suppress our feelings and judgments, we become them. When it comes to our relationships with our mothers, we act out this tendency by emulating the things we most hate about our mothers!

This is because although our mothers may no longer live in our homes, they still live in our heads, pushing us, criticizing us, chastising us. In one form or another, you will find that your mother is always present in those aspects of yourself that you have yet to embrace. Maybe you even gave birth to your mother, or married her. As long as you continue denying the negative feelings within yourself, the same patterns you established in your relationship with your mother will repeat in other relationships.

For most of us, our mother's love forms our initial understanding of what love is. The service and selfless giving that mothering universally represents are qualities that we all must learn to emulate on our journey to self-realization.

In order to love unconditionally, we must first learn to love and accept ourselves exactly as we are. How can we embrace others in their perfection if we cannot first see our own? If we reject certain aspects of ourselves, unconditional love toward others can never be anything more than a hollow facade. Similarly, in order to mother the world, we must first learn to mother ourselves — to find the beauty and perfection of our own individuality and rejoice in our unique way of being. Then acceptance and love of others will naturally overflow to our friends and family and ultimately to our community and the world.

When we cultivate true love of self, the love that is present within radiates out to all beings, all peoples, and Mother Earth. Many talk about what we should do to better the world — respect basic human rights, care for the environment, and so on. It is nice that we remind ourselves to do these things, but, ideally, wouldn't it be better if the desire to care and serve arose naturally and spontaneously within us? Then we wouldn't have to think: it would just be an action. Ultimately, our own inner healing will cause these qualities to flourish — not because we are *trying* to behave responsibly, but because out of an open heart we are joyfully taking responsibility for nurturing and protecting life.

An individual focused on giving unconditional love is

making the greatest contribution of all to the evolution of our planet. This gift to humanity comes through our own inner growth and advancement, a mothering of our self that births our own greatness, even as it brings out the greatness in others.

As you cultivate an unconditional love of yourself, you will find the unconditional love you seek to express for your children, parents, friends, and colleagues. You will become a universal mother: a mother of the world.

UNCONDITIONAL PARENTING

I refer to parenting from a place of love-consciousness as *unconditional parenting*, which means parenting without fear or fear-based attempts to control. It is neither lax nor careless nor based on pleasing or fear of losing the favor of a child. Real parental love knows how to set limits, establish boundaries, confront unsatisfactory situations, and guide a child's development with a steady, firm hand. Its nature is to surrender, trusting that things will unfold as they should. Free of the ego-based fear of making a mistake, it is neither overprotective nor overbearing.

If your child's behavior makes you feel insecure, or those around you make you mistrust yourself as a parent, stop. Don't torture yourself any longer. There is a direct path to transforming those feelings: going inward and finding the root of your self-doubt.

If your adolescent son is getting terrible grades, cutting school, and dabbling with alcohol and drugs, don't punish yourself or torture yourself by thinking things like *Maybe I didn't instill enough values in him* or *Maybe I didn't set enough limits.* I am sure you did the best you could with the resources that were available to you at the time. If you didn't love yourself, if you were insecure, if you yourself were needy for love, you probably couldn't give your child anything else. But today is a new day — now you can make new choices.

There is one thing our children always learn from us automatically, and that is our own example. They imitate us from an early age and learn to emulate our behavior, but they also register our feelings, even if we don't show them. It is not enough to tell them how they should behave — we must give the example; our words must be reflected in our actions. Then they will be received and understood on a much deeper level. If you have not cultivated self-esteem and self-love, telling your kids to take care of themselves will not be enough. One cares for oneself when one loves oneself; if you feel you are worthless, you become careless and will often look for experiences and situations that reaffirm that feeling.

If you worry that you haven't given them enough, my question would be, "Are you giving enough to yourself?" Are you listening to your internal needs? What do you think of yourself when you look in the mirror? Do you hear a voice of criticism or appreciation? You can be sure that is the same voice that raises your children; it is probably the voice your parents used to raise you.

You can heal the root of your self-rejection within by starting to consciously change your self-limiting behaviors, in small ways at first: start to love yourself in those places of insecurity and fear, and start to say yes to yourself. You will find that these subtle internal changes naturally start to show up in the way you treat others.

Many parents ask me how they can avoid passing their insecurities on to their children. The answer is, they cannot. Children will inevitably learn from their parents, even the things their parents try to keep from them. Yet this is simply part of life: your children are here to have a human experience. Don't try to shield them from life. Again, the best thing you can do to help your children overcome insecurity is to heal it within yourself. The best gift you can give your children is the inspiration of your own example. If you choose to love yourself, to heal yourself, your positive example will influence your children and help them take responsibility for their own issues.

We project our fears and frustrations onto our children: we don't want them to make the same mistakes we did, but because of this, we don't let them live. This suffocates our children — when you see yourself doing it, stop! Stop and connect with your heart. If, for example, your daughter is staying out late and you worry that she might be out drinking or even having unprotected sex, ask yourself, *What is happening in this moment that is so terrible?* Observe: maybe your mind will list a whole load of ideas and fears, but if you look deeper, you will realize they don't reflect reality in this moment. They are the product of your regrets from the past that are fueling a terrifying array of anxieties about the future — *What if she gets drunk and someone takes advantage of her? What if she gets pregnant? What if she gets addicted to alcohol? What will happen when she grows older? What if she doesn't have enough money? What if . . . ?* Focus on the present moment, on your actual surroundings right now. Remind yourself that your child is not you and in reality you have no idea how things will turn out.

Take a deep breath and ground yourself in trust in the innate perfection of the creative forces of the universe. Focus on the love. Trust that your perfect child is creating their life exactly as it should be.

Contemplation for Parents

- What insecurities do you have as a parent? What insecurities do you have inside yourself, as a person? Can you see a connection between the two?
- When you find yourself dwelling on thoughts of self-doubt, self-criticism, or worry about your child, bring yourself into the moment. Ideally, replace these thoughts with a facet (see Appendix 1, page 205). The mind can think only one thing at a time. By occupying your mind with the facets, you will be using the power of your intellect to uplift and inspire yourself, instead of using it for habitual thoughts that disempower you as well as your child.

THE END OF ACTIVE PARENTHOOD: EMPTY-NEST SYNDROME

There comes a time for every parent when our children no longer depend on us, and suddenly we no longer feel needed. They have their own world, their own lives, even their own families; their decisions no longer include us as ours do them. This is often when the questions start: *Now what? What am I worth now? Of what use am I? Who will take care of me when I am alone?* If this sounds like the game your head is playing with you in this moment, projecting concerns into the future, stop. This habit can only take you to a place of desolation and hopelessness. The scales will tip toward depression and inertia instead of expression and growth.

Start by appreciating the fact that you have completed your contribution to another human being, enabling them to create their own life, to open their wings and fly high in whatever they aspire to be.

As is the case in all stages of our lives, the subconscious mind is inventing fears and doubts that keep us clinging to our self-destructive patterns. Again, I invite you to simply focus on love, and then everything that comes from fear will start to disappear.

Contemplation for Empty-Nesters

When suddenly you find yourself facing the gap left when your children leave home, instead of focusing on what you have lost, open to the new possibilities your life is bringing. All the attention that you focused on nurturing and serving your children — now you can put it toward expanding your consciousness, loving yourself, and maybe pursuing adventures and hobbies or reviving old talents that you shelved during parenthood.

CHAPTER TWELVE

Intimate Relationships
Be the Partner You Wish to Have

*I*n our quest for wholeness, we often try to make up for our internal emptiness by seeking completion in another. Many of us have taken this to an extreme, believing that fulfillment is only possible in the arms of a soul mate.

Romance. The ultimate dream, especially if Hollywood has anything to do with it. The best thing that can ever happen to you: finding your dream partner. Yet until we heal our relationship with ourselves, we will see our own dissatisfaction reflected in our intimate relationships.

At first, things tend to go swimmingly, then with time, the judgments start to kick in. *Why doesn't he put the cap on the toothpaste?!* or *If he really loved me, he would pay me more attention*. Illusions are soon shattered, because as we look more closely at our partner, we begin to see things we don't like. In other words, we begin to see ourselves.

The problem is that in our obsession with finding external fulfillment, we neglect the most important relationship we have in our lives: our relationship with ourselves.

Our relationship with ourselves tends to be the one we attend to last. We often have our needs on the bottom of the list, after everyone else's. We think that loving ourselves is self-ish. Yet until we learn to love ourselves, our intimate relationships will be filled with need and codependency. Need is what leads to attachment. When we feel that we need someone or something in order to be happy, we become attached. With attachment comes the need to control. We feel we must control our circumstances, because our happiness depends on the outcomes we're attached to. We must control our partners, make sure they behave in the way that satisfies our need — our need to feel loved. The need to control leads to manipulation; all the little games we learn in order to get the other person to do what we want. Yet where is the love in all of this? Manipulation and control do not come from love; they come from fear.

The irony is, our partners are doing exactly the same thing. We play these games, modifying ourselves in order to please the other, abandoning what we really feel out of fear of rejection. We all live in limitation and dissatisfaction, thinking that if we allow ourselves to be exactly as we are, we will be rebuked by those we love. Yet everyone else is doing exactly the same!

When you love yourself, your relationships become honest and transparent, because you lose the fear of loss. You allow yourself to be real, to show yourself exactly as you are, and in doing so, you give your partner the freedom to do the same. This honesty builds trust, which is the basis of a truly loving relationship. With self-love, you lose the fear of rejection and the need to control. All behaviors that create separation and judgment fall away in the light of self-love; as we embrace ourselves, we are able to embrace our partners, holding them in their greatness. When we feel complete within ourselves, we no longer feel the absence of the other when they are not present, so the need to control them disappears naturally. With this sense of self-sufficiency comes great freedom and the ability to truly enjoy each other's presence.

We tend to think that if we let go of the attachment to our loved ones, we will lose them, but actually the opposite is true. When you love without conditions, even if your partner is not by your side you will feel closer to them than ever before. For you will have found them within yourself.

MAN IN THE MIRROR

Although we often don't want to admit it, the problems we have with our partners are usually problems we have with ourselves.

I used to habitually feel that my partners could not commit. I created relationships with men who were on the rebound or, earlier in my life, men who were still involved with other women. I continually demanded that they love me more, that they commit to our relationship. Yet at the first sign of commitment, I was the one who abandoned ship. Whenever a potential partner appeared who was eager to get married, settle down, and have children, I couldn't run away fast enough, my head full of excuses: that he was boring, not attractive enough, and so on. The list of what was wrong with them was endless, while the ones who couldn't and wouldn't commit always seemed so perfect. Needless to say, when I began to look inward, it became abundantly clear that the person who wouldn't commit was me.

We are always in a relationship with ourselves, our partners mirroring back to us the behaviors of our own that we don't like. We are quick to deny this, whipping out the list of things our partners do wrong, which of course bear no resemblance to the way we behave.

Yet before we rush to dismiss this idea, let's look a bit more carefully. What does your partner's behavior make you feel? What is the internal judgment you have about the things that annoy you? Why was I always the mistress and not the wife? When I felt my partner's lack of commitment, it angered me and made me want to change him, yet as soon as that commitment was required of me, I was the one incapable of taking responsibility.

One thing is certain: if you don't like what you see externally, you need to remove it internally. Then what you see in your partner will change. Once you start to love yourself, once you start to understand the source of your foibles and to accept them, they will fall away naturally. You will find yourself before a new reflection, a loving reflection. This doesn't necessarily mean you will change partners; it means that by changing yourself, you will be creating a space for your perception of your partner to change.

If you are dissatisfied with some aspect of yourself, you will create that same dissatisfaction externally until you transform it within yourself. When you take responsibility for loving that aspect of yourself, you will no longer react to it in your partner. You will look at it with love and see your underlying fears and judgments with love. You will no longer be attached to the idea of your partner being a certain way. You will be amazed to see how people change as a result of your own inner transformation.

This is evolution at work, expressed through personal relationships: when you observe your mirrors and take your feelings inward, the opportunities for growth are infinite. Dare to have this internal adventure, and watch as the external dramas dissolve, as if by magic. You will find yourself surrounded by brilliant mirrors, reflecting unconditional love.

SPOUSE

Meet somebody, fall in love, get married. That's how it goes, right? Then what? We hear of astronomical divorce rates, couple therapy, and extramarital affairs, but we also hear of the picture-perfect fifty-year happy marriages. What is this need to get married, and why do we think it will fulfill us?

If I were going to be cynical, I might say that the institution of marriage stems from people's insecurity and their resulting need to create a feeling of safety with contracts and promises; I might say that marriage is a man-made constraint that comes from fear and thus is fragile. We feel the need to make the other commit so we can control them, so we can be sure they will stay by our side and make us feel safe. Often marriage also stems from a need to receive public approval or to fulfill a childhood fairy-tale fantasy that we have had pushed down our throats, like the chicken soup we were told could cure a cold.

Yet I don't wish to make it all appear so bleak. In a marriage between two people who love each other unconditionally, there is no need to tie the other person down or try to control them in any way; unconditional love gives the other the freedom of expression that we all wish for — the freedom to be ourselves. What greater love is there than that? If you really love someone, how could you want them to be anyone else? This type of marriage flourishes and blossoms into two individuals supporting each other in realizing their own potential.

When we start being honest with ourselves, honesty begins to grow in our relationships. This is when the bond between us and our partners is truly tested. I have been visited by many couples who have been married for decades and want to experience the process of inner growth together. When they visit my center, they learn to express themselves and often end up sharing things that they have avoided saying for years. It is wonderful to see how this honesty breathes new life and intimacy into relationships that have become strained and distant. By confronting the fear of harming each other, they return home rejuvenated, more united and loving than ever.

But for some couples this process proves more challenging. For example, a married couple, both experienced psychologists who were deeply committed to the Isha System and their own healing, recently came to participate in a long-term deep-healing program in my center. When the wife began to grow and to express the things she had not dared to say before, when she stopped treating her husband like a child and started voicing her own needs, her husband immediately wanted to leave and terminate the program. His wife was no longer falling for the same manipulative games, and he suddenly felt insecure. When this happens we have the choice to go inward and find true security or to continue avoiding ourselves and find a new external crutch. Some days passed, and he went deeper, ultimately deciding to stay on and to confront his fears and let go of the abandonment that had crippled him for so long.

Our need to make our partner vow to love us eternally comes from our own desperate need to be loved. This need will continue unsated until we come to love ourselves. The impulse to control others comes from our lack of self-love. We have learned to reject ourselves so much that we have become slaves of outside approval; our sense of worth depends almost entirely on the opinions of those around us. This is so even for seemingly successful, powerful people; if their confidence lies in their success or public standing, where will it go if those things are taken away?

Marriage isn't a remedy for insecurity. The only true remedy for insecurity is self-love — going beyond the fears and doubts of the mind and developing an awareness of the underlying security that is our very being. True love, unconditional love, breaks all boundaries, boxes, and ideas. It is the unlimited nature of being; it is life itself.

SETTLE FOR NOTHING LESS THAN COMPLETE HONESTY AND TRANSPARENCY

We all lie. We lie to receive approval, to manipulate other people's opinions of us. How contradictory it is: we are taught as children that we must always tell the truth, that we shouldn't lie, yet society teaches us to lie "appropriately" — in order to avoid conflict, to be polite, to get what we want. This is especially true in our intimate relationships.

This reminds me of one rather dysfunctional aspect of my family. Back in the '80s it seemed as if everyone smoked except for my mother and grandmother. The presence of a cigarette was enough to bring them into compulsive coughing fits and spontaneous watering of the eyes, and the whole family had been trained like Pavlov's dogs to tut appropriately in the presence of a smoker. The problem was that everyone else in the family actually did smoke — I, my boyfriend, my father, my brother, and his wife — and after our simulated tutting we would remove ourselves as a unit to the bathroom to have a surreptitious cigarette, followed by the hasty application of mouth spray, perfume, or whatever was needed to camouflage the smell of cigarette. We had been carrying out this charade for so long and to such an extent that we actually perceived it to be quite normal. We were oblivious to the fact that we were all terrified of my grandmother and mother, desperately masking our addictions in order to receive their approval!

Lies are self-abandonment. Each lie represents a place where we avoid showing ourselves exactly as we are, and so ultimately they come from fear — fear of being rejected, fear of feeling unloved. We put on social masks, presenting a false persona to the world, the person we think we should appear to be. Yet in doing so, we deny parts of ourselves, which either become secret obsessions or suppressed emotions resulting in resentment and disillusionment.

How often do we sacrifice sincerity with our partners in

order to avoid conflict or hide some aspect of ourselves? Our need for approval often trumps our commitment to being truthful, but self-abandonment is a high price to pay to maintain an appearance of harmony.

If we feel the need to hide something from our partners, it is because on some level we know that our actions are not based in love and growth. But secrets in intimate relationships become open wounds that fester, preventing the relationships from ever being healthy. The biggest toll they take is on us, because our concealments are always there, lurking behind every corner and inflicting us with a pervasive sense of unease, guilt, and shame.

Make it your policy to never hide your behaviors from your partner. Make *Full Disclosure* your mantra. Once you decide to put honesty and transparency above the need for approval or the need to manipulate your partner, everything will begin to change. You'll be amazed at how much your self-esteem will improve along with your relationship.

HOW TO MOVE FROM CONDITIONAL LOVE TO UNCONDITIONAL LOVE

How can we tell if our intimate relationships are based on need or something deeper? Here I share some common indicators of codependency and other behaviors that erode goodwill and harmony in relationships. Ask yourself if these scenarios describe your relationship, and then read my suggestions for how to transform these behaviors into a more loving way of interacting.

SCENARIO: *You lie to your partner.*

Lies may range from little things, such as "Yes, honey, I love your chicken casserole," to more important ones, such as telling your spouse you have to work late when in reality you are going to meet a lover. But whether they're white lies or whoppers, they're a sign of a relationship based in need — the need to receive the approval of the other.

SOLUTION: *Be honest.*

Love is always truthful. Lying comes from fear. If you want a loving relationship, the truth is the only option. Always.

SCENARIO: *You try to control and change your partner.*

The need to modify them comes from your own expectations of how you think they should behave in order for you to feel supported and loved. This comes from not taking responsibility for your own security.

SOLUTION: *Let go.*

When you see yourself manipulating or being overbearing, stop. Bring yourself into the moment and think to yourself, *Oh, I can let that go.* Go inward and focus on loving yourself. Then the need to control your partner will fall away.

SCENARIO: *Your conversations always turn into arguments.*

You may find that the smallest disagreements spark disproportionate arguments in your relationship, that before you have finished giving your point of view, your partner is already reacting from a past expectation of what you are thinking or feeling, and vice versa.

SOLUTION: *Listen.*

When your partner is talking to you, really listen to what they are saying, *especially if you don't agree or if it makes you angry.* You will find that the things you least want to hear can help you grow the most. You don't have to agree in order to listen, and by listening you are not automatically making the other person right, but you are opening up to receive what they have to show you. When you listen, you learn more about the other person, but, most importantly, you learn more about yourself.

SCENARIO: *You resent your partner.*

If you do not express your feelings openly with your partner, resentment will begin to grow within you. This resentment will then be triggered by the silliest little things. During an argument, you will whip out the list of everything you feel resentful about.

SOLUTION: *Be vulnerable.*

A truly loving relationship will bear the test of the truth. Be honest about what you are feeling, and you will soon see the true nature of your relationship. Tell your partner how you feel — on a regular basis, whenever feelings come up. Don't try to change them; express your feelings with the goal of being totally transparent, of showing yourself exactly as you are. Recognize the fear at the root of your tendency not to speak up, and allow yourself to feel it. By doing so, you will begin to release the emotional charge that causes resentment, and to replace it with love.

The wonderful thing about these recommendations is that they only take one person to work! Don't fall into the trap of thinking, *I can't share my feelings with him because he never listens* or *I'll be honest with her if she is honest with me*. If your relationship is truly based in mutual love and respect, it will only become more intimate, more fulfilling if you adopt these behaviors. If, on the other hand, the love really has gone, then the relationship will probably end soon. Yet ask yourself this: when faced with the truth, would you really want to spend your life with someone who doesn't love you? Once you start being honest enough to confront that reality, you will already be well on the way to loving yourself. You will find that this more than compensates for the loss of an ultimately unfulfilling relationship.

Once you decide to put honesty and transparency above the need for approval or the need to manipulate your partner, everything will begin to change.

KNOWING WHEN IT IS TIME TO LEAVE

Unconditional love must start with self-love. If you abandon yourself in order to maintain a relationship, you are not being unconditionally loving — you are clinging to an external form that may no longer serve you or your partner. A truly loving relationship will always lead to more growth.

Many years ago I started a relationship with someone who, unbeknownst to me, had a record of substance abuse. I soon found out about her history, and then I realized that she had stopped taking drugs because I was the new addiction. When the excitement of romance and sexual attraction stopped fulfilling her internal emptiness, the drugs started to reappear. I made many attempts to help my partner overcome this drug problem, until I realized that in reality I, too, was struggling with addiction: I was addicted to saving. Instead of confronting my own internal emptiness and loving myself unconditionally, I had focused all my attention on someone who clearly looked worse off than I was, so I could feel good about myself.

I also felt like a victim within this relationship. Because I could not trust my partner, I didn't feel valued: why wasn't I more important than the drug? Finally, the penny dropped and I realized that I had to make myself important. In that moment, when I decided to create a loving relationship with myself, the external relationship fell away, because the mirror was not reflecting the beauty I saw in myself. I decided to leave.

Your situation might not be as obvious as mine was, or it might be more extreme. If you are unhappy in your relationship and not sure whether to stick around or move on, ask yourself, *Is this relationship serving my growth? Is this relationship supporting me in finding my own greatness, in loving and valuing myself? Do I feel loved for who I am or am I trying to meet the expectations of my partner?* If a relationship makes you feel small, it does not serve your growth. If a relationship makes you feel dependent on another, or if you are abandoning yourself in order to make your partner feel comfortable, it is based in need. If you find yourself in this kind of relationship, start speaking your truth and being yourself. If your partner doesn't feel comfortable with this, they will have two choices: to accept you as you are, or to move on.

Contemplation

- Are you waiting for the perfect partner? Instead of looking outside, focus on falling in love with yourself. Be the perfect partner to yourself, appreciating yourself, inspiring yourself, giving yourself the trust and support you seek.

- If you are in a relationship, observe where you abandon yourself in order to please the other. Speak your truth even if you feel afraid of being rejected. Speaking out may sometimes feel scary, but in the long run it will bring nothing but greater honesty and transparency to your relationship. True intimacy cannot be reached if we are wearing a mask: if our true selves are hidden behind what we think is appropriate, we distance ourselves from the people we love the most.

- When you see something you don't like in your partner, take it inward. Ask yourself, *How does it make me feel when he/she does that?* Instead of trying to change your partner, tell them how you feel, with the intention of letting those feelings go. You will be amazed to discover how many of the things you judge or reject in your partner are actually aspects of yourself. If you use them to go inward and heal, you can transform the things you dislike about your relationship into unexpected gifts: opportunities to heal and to grow.

CHAPTER THIRTEEN

Redefining and Realizing Success in Work

*H*ave you ever reached a point in your life when you felt you had everything, yet there was still something missing? In my twenties, my external success should have been enough, yet I wasn't happy. The things I had accumulated, my social status and professional achievements, all seemed too fragile, too empty, to be all there was. I thirsted for something more, but that something was intangible.

We have learned to measure our worth by our external achievements, yet no scale could be more superficial. One can be rich and famous, with countless admirers, with the most extreme of material excesses, and yet not find peace. We see this in so many icons of wealth and fame whose personal dissatisfaction ultimately leads them to disillusionment. The fulfillment we seek cannot be derived from outside accomplishments; the yearning of the heart is internal. The external quest can be fun, but it cannot bring freedom.

For me, success is love-consciousness, a life without fear, a life that inspires others to aspire toward the same. What do *you* really want? Is the appearance of success enough, or does it leave you yearning for something deeper?

True success is defined by what we are being in each moment, not by what we are doing. If we are internally abundant, giving from a place of love, and valuing ourselves, we will find a much more meaningful definition of success.

> *True success is defined by what we are being in each moment, not by what we are doing.*

Once you have the internal experience of love-consciousness and peace, everything external you could have ever dreamed of — and more — comes to you, in abundance and without strain.

Because you are not attached.

As long as our happiness depends on the external, we can never be truly free: we will remain slaves to the outside, dependent on the approval and appreciation of others.

In order to free ourselves from this dependency, we must familiarize ourselves with the love that lies within, which no one can ever take away, instead of entertaining our fear-based thoughts, which limit and repress — the relentless criticism inside the mind, the regrets of what has passed, and the resistance to what will come. To start going inward is the first step. Choose to give thanks for what is, instead of choosing to feel resentment, to fight, criticize, and destroy. Remember that whatever you focus on grows. What do you want to flourish in your life? Focus on cultivating what you want. You will be amazed how quickly things begin to change.

AIMING FOR GOALS OR
LIVING IN THE PRESENT?

I have often met professionals who struggle to reconcile living in the present moment with focusing on achieving their goals.

I see no such dilemma. Excellence in any area of life, and definitely in any enterprise or career path, comes from being fully present, giving the best of ourselves in each moment, and being aware of the details that others may have overlooked. We all have goals, but if our goals make us constantly focus on a future moment, they are ultimately distractions. Be clear in your objectives, but give 100 percent in this moment. You're not at the end of the path until you get there. In the meantime, discover the joy of the journey.

You can't structure your life around achieving a goal. Just when you're reaching your objective, the winds change and suddenly your course is different. You have to flow; you have to move. You have to be open to the possibility that maybe what you think you want isn't going to bring you joy, that in reality any need for things to be a certain way is ultimately limiting.

This perspective does not run counter to the business framework; on the contrary, any group that focuses on love-consciousness will experience tremendous synergy and unity. If every member of a team is working with a clear vision of union, communication and cooperation come naturally and spontaneously. Individuals living and working from a place of joy create a more efficient and enjoyable workplace.

Be open to everything. We all think we know what's best, but the joy of life lies in its unpredictability. Empires are built, and then they collapse. Everything in this world is fragile — except that which is real, that which never changes but just becomes more and more and more. Be open. Organize your life, by all means, but cultivate the capacity to flow, to let go, to change, to let go of your mind and fall into your heart.

As the world thunders past me, my thighs aching after 120 kilometers and ten hours of straddling what now feels like the most uncomfortable horse in the world, the same thought I had at this stage of my last race appears: *Why am I doing this?*

Endurance racing is intense. Spanning 160 kilometers, the races challenge the horse and rider to the extreme. When I'm in the thick of it, there is a point when my body always screams, *Why?!*

Then I remember why: it's because I love it. Sometimes it's tiring, but that's part of what fascinates me: the challenge, the excitement and delight of each moment, moving toward the goal but remaining anchored in the present, rider and horse as one, my awareness fused with this magnificent, powerful creature, its strength and resilience a thing of great beauty.

The health and pacing of the animal form an essential part of the classification process: after each lap, the horses are monitored by veterinarians. Their heart rate must fall below sixty beats per minute within the twenty minutes following each lap. Those that do not pass these vigorous vet checks are disqualified. So the sport is about caring as much as it's about racing, about giving as well as receiving — if I don't give my horse the best care leading up to and during the race, he will not pass the vet checks or carry me to victory. So I must carry the health and well-being of the horse as much as he must carry me.

If during the race I am constantly worrying, *Will he pass the vet check? What if he trips on a stone? Will he be sound for the next lap?* then I'm not present to deal with problems as they arise. I am focused on an outcome instead of enjoying the race itself. When we are surrendered to each moment, we are beyond results, even beyond pain; we are not suffering in the anticipation of a future occurrence.

STRESS IN THE WORKPLACE

In times of uncertainty, it is easy to work ourselves into a panic. The looming threat of losing our security, be it real or imaginary, generates high levels of stress. We might be going through a divorce or a time of uncertainty in the workplace, with layoffs at the office. Often we subconsciously exaggerate the gravity of our situation. Obsessed with fearing the worst, we let this obsession stifle the flexibility that these unpredictable times require more than ever.

Everything we feel inside ourselves we project onto our surroundings. Often the conflicts we have at home are triggered by the stress we bring from work, and vice versa. We cannot relieve our stress by making external changes or solving problems, for when one issue has passed another appears. The solution must come from within. Allow yourself to feel what is going on and respond to your inner needs without carrying them around as self-inflicted stress, adding to the burden of the stress already imposed by the demands of your job.

Imagine you arrive at the office, carrying all the problems

you had at home on your back. Maybe you had an argument at breakfast; maybe one of the kids was sick and had to be taken to the doctor; maybe you had a bit too much to drink the night before and are not feeling your best. You might not want to talk to anyone with all that tension inside, and your responsibilities at work only serve to increase that tension. What can you do about all this?

Depending on your temperament, and maybe your position at work, you might give way to some counterproductive form of expression: an explosion of anger, an argument, a scream, punching a desk. Or maybe you will just repress the feelings, trying not to bring your personal problems into the workplace. Neither of these two responses is ideal. Unexpressed emotions accumulate in the nervous system; the body feels them, and they can eventually manifest as physical illnesses. On the other hand, if you unload your stress onto others, you are not contributing to a healthy work environment. So what can you do with all this emotional charge?

Right there in the office, rather than passively pretending that everything is fine, you can take any of the following constructive actions to release anger or sadness. You can release anger by screaming or beating an inanimate object (preferably something soft), while you can move sadness by crying; you can do both of these things in a harmless way that hurts no one. Feeling angry at work? Go to the bathroom, roll up a hand towel, and move the intensity of your emotion by screaming into the towel. Do you feel frustrated, want to cry? Don't swallow your tears; let them flow. Release the feeling so it doesn't become repressed resentment held in your chest, and your heart will be left open to feel fresh in every moment.

There are other ways to release frustration too: if you can, when the day is getting the better of you, take a brisk walk around the block, or even just along the corridor or up and down the staircase. If you find yourself craving a cigarette or some comfort food, stop for a mo-

Feeling angry at work? Go to the bathroom, roll up a hand towel, and move the intensity of your emotion by screaming into the towel.

ment and ask yourself, *What am I feeling?* Connect with the feeling first, even if you ultimately have that cigarette or snack. At least you will have given yourself a moment to release the charge that triggers the behavior, and with time the intensity of the craving will diminish.

If your tension stems from feelings you have toward someone you work with, walk toward them instead of turning away, and speak your truth. To let go of the past, express what you have been feeling toward them. Move the charge it gener-ates in you, and release it.

ENLIGHTENED COMMUNICATION IN THE WORKPLACE

At work we often think we shouldn't express what we feel for fear of hurting or alienating someone. We say, "Hello. How nice to see you," while internally we are thinking, *I hate him, but I have to work with him every day, so I'll just smile and say, "How are you?" when in reality I don't care how he is.*

Being polite and friendly without feeling is not real. Because it comes from the head, it's intellectual, disconnected; the heart is not present in the feeling, and the other person always knows it.

Recently, lies have come to light that have exposed corruption and manipulation on a global scale in many different situations. WikiLeaks has played a prominent role in this trend, yet I see it as a reflection of the increasing honesty that is coming on a personal scale, in the lives of people around the world who are beginning to go inward and face the truth. Only truth can set us free; truth is the language of love-consciousness. As we become more truthful, the world we live in will begin to reflect that honesty. We can march for equality, demand more of our politicians, and work to expose injustice, but we can best contribute to an honest and fair society by becoming more transparent in our own lives.

In the workplace, we tend to ignore our emotions and pretend everything is fine. That way, we avoid disagreements and live in a state of apparent conviviality, but beneath lies all the frustration, all the rage, often toward the people we have to work with every day.

We need to express ourselves with clarity, to be real; if we don't, we start to hate ourselves. The mind says, *But I'm afraid! I might hurt someone!* or *I might make enemies at work* or *I might get fired*. But if you continually swallow your discontent and bury your grievances, you are already hurting someone: you're hurting yourself.

Truth flies the highest. Truth always generates unity. Protective dishonesty increases fear and generates separation. Make a habit of voicing your concerns with your coworkers in a compassionate way, open to hearing what they have to say in response. When they see you free of fears, judgments, and resentment, your relationships with them will start to change, and soon you will feel much closer to them.

Truth flies the highest.

Another tendency on the job is to get so caught up in the routine of our days that we forget to ever say anything nice. How many bosses take their subordinates for granted, forgetting to ac-knowledge the countless ways those assistants make their jobs — and consequently their lives — easier? Conversely, assis-tants often get resentful about their lowly positions, forgetting that their roles are just as integral as those of the managers and grumbling when anything additional is asked of them, rather than welcoming the chance to learn something new or chal-lenge themselves.

When we focus on our difficulties, complaints form the base of our workplace conversations. But we can counteract this tendency by consciously offering praise, the appreciation that opens the doors to the infinite. Has your boss just given you a new type of assignment that offers more creativity than your usual humdrum tasks? Tell her you're excited about it, and thank her. Has your assistant done a great job typing up the minutes from the board meeting? Tell him so. Do you like the shoes that Carol from HR is wearing? Compliment her. By giving praise or compliments, you can completely change the energy in the room. Selflessly acknowledging those around you offers the added bonus of making you feel happier too. Get in the habit of saying something nice to someone at work every day, and you'll discover a new experience based in warmth and love, beyond your wildest workaday dreams.

Contemplation

Every situation provides opportunities to be conscious.

- In the office, look for ways to give, instead of focusing on what you are getting. Focus on the joy of serving within your role in the workplace. Remember, he or she who gives, wins.
- Where can you work more as a unit and be part of a team working toward a common goal? Focus on listening, especially to those who usually annoy you, or the ones you may feel resentment toward.
- If you don't like someone's attitude, tell them instead of complaining behind their back. You will start to find that your criticisms can actually be useful, encouraging others to improve as human beings and in their roles at work.

PART THREE

Remedies for the Afflictions of Modern Living

*T*he pace of our world seems to have increased exponentially in recent years. Our heads feel full of an unbearable chatter of voices, a cacophony of reproaches and expectations that reach beyond what is humanly possible to achieve — *You have to do this* and *Why don't we do that?* In our haste to live up to the demands and expectations of those around us, we often allow the pressure of those many demands to get the better of us.

Sometimes we feel exhausted even before we get out of bed in the morning; a series of emotions that leave us confused and intolerant are detonated. We have so many internal demands that when our children, spouses, or bosses ask us for something more, we explode. Then, as a result, we feel the added burden of guilt and regret for having exploded. We want to excel but we don't know how to find the middle ground, within which we can confront whatever life brings without feeling weight upon our backs or anguish in our throats. We oscillate between exasperation and dejected resignation, unable to enjoy what we have in our lives right now.

This description may sound extreme, yet I hear these sentiments surprisingly often. Faced with ever-increasing external demands, we subject ourselves to a constant barrage of internal emotional and mental attacks, which manifest in many different ways: as depression, insomnia, and panic attacks, among other things. In our relationships we have conflicts with our partners. We experience distorted communication with our children and a constant fearful need to control them as they push against boundaries, challenging our authority and exploring a world that seems increasingly unpredictable and dangerous. Our attempts to protect them from harm leave a sense of futility as we are paralyzed with fear and frustration. In a world where it often feels as though we no longer speak the language, we don't know what to do or how to respond, how to establish a channel of communication, a common thread.

I am here to remind you that you can choose love and peace in every moment, joyfully, no matter what life throws at you. In these final chapters, I offer simple tools you can use to ease the pressure created by the demands of modern life, and embody peace. I want to show you how to get to a place of no more struggling, no more seeking.

CHAPTER FOURTEEN

Conscious Vacations and BEcations
Antidotes to the Daily Grind

When we feel the demands of the world upon our shoulders, it is essential to stay flexible, to flow, connected with the most essential and fundamental aspects of our being. This is the key to staying clear and alert when confronted with difficult decisions.

Of course, this is easier said than done. For many of us, from the moment we wake up to the moment we drift off to sleep at night we are attending to the needs of our children, the demands and dynamics of our work, and the chores involved with maintaining a household. How can we keep the tenets of love-consciousness in the forefront of our psyches?

Until we learn to infuse our day-to-day lives with love-consciousness, we are like big, clunky old diesel trucks. We are fueled with a gunky compound derived from the deepest layers of emotional residue. This fuel is an outmoded technology inherited from centuries past, rooted in a sense of scarcity and derived through conflict and ecological devastation. Although we may start each day with a full tank, our fuel isn't efficient and doesn't get us very far before the demands of our lives run it down to empty, leaving us depleted and the world around us polluted by our emissions of resentment and mistrust.

But in this new millennium we have options. We can instead become zero-emission vehicles that run on pure love. We can start out each day feeling refreshed, as though we could drive to the moon and back without running out of fuel. Wherever we go, we emit nothing toxic, only love. No matter how much ground we have to cover on a given day — no matter how many demands are placed on us by our jobs or our families — we always have more left in our tank at the end of the day, and we can recharge our batteries at any time by simply plugging ourselves into our eternal source.

In addition to all the practices and insights I've shared in this book so far, I have two more suggestions to help you become like a zero-emission lovemobile instead of a stinky old jalopy: conscious vacations and BEcations.

Take a Conscious Vacation

Time off. The high point of the year, the oasis of freedom in a desert of routine. Vacations make the mundane more bearable, shining a light on the horizon, something to look forward to. Yet with vacations come travel preparations, family gatherings, and extra expenses — their own set of demands, expectations, and chores.

The kids are out of school. Maybe we can spend our time with them, or maybe we must find child care for them because we have obligations at work. Maybe we will go to the beach, the mountains, or some other exotic location, or perhaps we will stay at home and plan day trips with the family.

Vacations are new opportunities to share, but they can easily become yet another reason to feel pressured as we demand too much from ourselves. To get the most out of your vacation time, use it as an opportunity to fortify your relationship with yourself. As a natural result, your relationships with your nearest and dearest will also be strengthened. Use these days together to try different ways of doing things. Here are some ideas that will undoubtedly lead to different results. Best of all, the following activities cost nothing and require no advance planning.

- Try being more sensitive with your family, and more aware of your surroundings. Start by committing time each day to connecting with yourself, devoting an hour a day to the practice of the facets of the Isha System (see Appendix 1, page 205) or the spiritual practice of your choice. Then bring that self-awareness into your interactions with your family, listening to yourself, staying present with yourself and aware of your own reactions and feelings in your exchanges with them. When you are in touch with yourself, it is hard to be insensitive with others. It is when we are distracted by the fears and worries of the mind, or engrossed in some activity to escape ourselves, that our interactions become brusque and our responses disproportionately harsh.

    When a loved one comes to speak with you, be it

your child, girlfriend, husband, or mother, give them your full attention. Make eye contact, find something to appreciate, ask the other person how they are feeling. Don't assume anything — if you are not sure what they are saying, ask, and focus on really listening to their response, connecting with them from the heart. You will find that by paying attention to these little details, your family relationships will become more intimate, more honest, and more loving.

- Focus on appreciating and giving thanks for the small things in life, the beauty of the world around you, the spontaneous laughter shared with a friend. You could even try challenging yourself to see how many times in a given day you can express this appreciation out loud: if someone or something brings you joy, thank them or compliment them, or comment on the beauty you see around you. Hearing and seeing your appreciation of the world and of your loved ones will set a good example for those around you, especially your children, and will make them feel closer to you. Love-consciousness is contagious!

- Dare to do something that you haven't done for some time with your children or partner or pet; surprise them with an adventure that will leave a memory of good times shared, adventures that don't even cost any money. Use your imagination or ask them for ideas. We tend to plan around consumption, yet there is so much natural wonder around us wherever we look; sometimes the most amazing things in life are so close we don't even notice them. If you live in the city, can you get out of town or at least go to the park or the nearest nature preserve? Do you remember what brought you wonder when you were a child? Remember how fascinating it was to just sit still and watch something, totally present in the experience? We tend to incorporate our kids into more adult forms of entertainment, but maybe there is something simpler that can unite us all. Try building a sand castle together, or playing hide and seek, or picking flowers or fruit. Or maybe you could take a nighttime adventure to gaze at the stars and see how many constellations you can find — or better yet, make up your own!

When you devote some or all of your vacation time to stepping outside of your everyday demands and into complete presence with your loved ones, you will find it easier to connect with them emotionally, reducing conflicts, dropping fears, ideas, and masks, discovering the deepest form of love that flows between us all, just because. You will find that when you focus on appreciating and giving thanks, love flows more naturally in its expression.

Taking a conscious vacation is one of the best gifts you can give yourself and your loved ones. Focus on appreciating this experience with them to the fullest.

TRY A BECATION

If you ever feel that things are getting the better of you, I propose that you try a new concept: a *BEcation*. What we really need is time to be. Time to listen to ourselves, to disconnect from the constant doing of daily life, to do nothing at all. We are usually so busy that we have lost touch with our inner voice, we have forgotten what we really want.

How do you take a BEcation? It's simple: set aside some time just to be with yourself. To go inward and listen. To feel whatever might come up, be it peace and joy, or anxiety and insecurity. Being with yourself naturally makes you more conscious. Being present in the moment, silently observing what is happening in your surroundings, brings greater clarity into your life. It helps you dissociate from the chaotic thoughts based in fear and criticism that so often dominate our decisions. It helps you discern the difference between the fears of the mind and the truth of the heart. It helps you get your priorities in order.

You spend so much time doing — can't you spare a little time just for yourself? Here are some practical guidelines for taking a BEcation.

- A BEcation could last a day or a couple of days...or it could become a regular part of your routine — each Sunday afternoon, for example.
- Use your BEcation as time to disconnect from distractions. Turn off the TV, resist the urge to pick up a book, try just being with yourself. The facets explained in Appendix 1 (page 205) are an ideal tool for cultivating this awareness of self, and a perfect BEcation could simply involve practicing the facets in any number of settings — with your eyes open or closed, in your favorite chair, wrapped up warm in bed on a

rainy day, or even taking the dog for a walk. The important thing is that you take time to be with yourself.

• Plan your BEcation in advance: mark the day or time on your calendar. This way it will be easier to stick with your commitment to yourself, and not postpone this time by distracting yourself with other things the mind deems more important. There is nothing more important than our relationship with ourselves, yet it is so easy to forget this and get lost in doing. Taking time for yourself is anything but selfish, as it replenishes you and puts you in a better state of mind, allowing you to rise to the challenges of your days with more peace, clarity, and compassion.

Conscious vacations and BEcations instill a profound level of self-trust that nurtures your inner self and begins to guide your decisions with greater clarity. The result will be better communication and more understanding between you and your children, your partner, and your colleagues. They also help you stabilize your relationship with the now. You will begin to see the now as a fertile garden, and during these times of recreation, you will be planting seeds that will bloom into flowers and fruits that bring new colors and hues to your days and provide nourishment to your feelings. By setting aside and utilizing this space to rest and grow, you will bring new wisdom into your life: the wisdom of your own inner truth, which comes from listening to your heart.

CHAPTER FIFTEEN

Appreciating Yourself and Your Surroundings
The Antidote to Insecurity and Loneliness

*I*n the world today, an unprecedented number of people struggle with feelings of insecurity and loneliness. People of all walks of life and age groups ask me how to cope with these debilitating feelings. I think one of the reasons this has become so common is that many of us don't give time to our relationship with ourselves: we don't value the beauty of our internal presence. We have lost the ability to enjoy being with ourselves and have become dependent on external distraction. The solution, then, is to go inward. Here are some reflections on these challenging emotions and suggestions for exploring the self to move beyond them.

INSECURITY

How can we overcome the feeling of insecurity in an uncertain world? How can we find true stability in the shifting sands of modern times? The truth is, security can be found only where it has always been found: within.

If ever you feel insecure, don't reject the feeling — it will only come back to haunt you. If you ignore a child, he will linger, begging to be loved; if you ignore a part of yourself, it will remain in the back of your mind, like a lie that you can hide but never forget.

Confronting the parts of yourself that you judge is scary. In doing so, you are admitting that the mask you have presented to society is a lie. You are dropping the crutches you have used to feel strong, and there will be a moment when you doubt your ability to walk alone. But if you want to be free of insecurity, this is a process you will have to face.

Before I began my journey of self-discovery, my insecurity was debilitating. I constantly felt shy and intimidated, but I had an idea of who I should be, so I used to hide my fragility behind the facade of my confident and outgoing appearance. Yet behind that facade, I had to live with the truth. To some extent, we all do this. We have an idea of how we should present ourselves to others, but as long as we depend on the shifting opinions of a changeable world, we will live in fear. The only way to overcome this fear is to shed the shells we have erected to protect ourselves, for they so easily become prisons.

This process of self-acceptance is an act of love. It is the greatest gift you can give to yourself. Be gentle when you do it — don't punish yourself for feeling insecure, or for what you perceive as your shortcomings. If a child is afraid, do you punish her? No, you love her, you talk to her, you console her. Yet with ourselves, we are violent and unforgiving; we don't tolerate our mistakes. In order to find internal security, we must learn to love and trust ourselves.

We need to learn to accept our every aspect, not from a place of resignation or feeling as though we've failed but by learning to love the child within and seeing beyond the aspects that no longer serve us.

When you become aware of an aspect of yourself that you have learned to hide, move toward it. Don't continue covering it with more layers of personality. If you feel uncertain about how to complete a new assignment given to you at work, ask for help. Don't compromise the result of your project out of fear of looking uncertain. If you have a strong temper, embrace it! Your temper is a natural aspect of your humanity, and if you learn to love it, you can use that passion to inspire those around you to achieve more! We think love is sweet and meek, but love can be forceful: it can shake passivity and comfort into action. By repressing your anger, you are also repressing your power, your passion, your leadership qualities.

Body image is another area in which we tend to have a great deal of insecurity. Living in South America, I have noticed that Latinos seem to be better at embracing their bodies than people of other Western cultures. In Brazil, for example, women with lots of cellulite go to the beach in thongs. They don't seem to care, embracing their bodies as they are, whereas if they were Australian or American, they would probably lie in the sand in a wetsuit before going out in a thong! The sooner you recognize and embrace the parts of your body that you don't like, the sooner you will be free of the dislike. For underneath our shame about our bodies lies a fear of not being loved. And when you embrace your fear, recognizing it for what it is, the illusion it has created falls. Then what is left? Love. As with clouds moving across the sun, when the illusions pass, the light shines through. Confront your fears with love — don't reject them or avoid them; if you do, the clouds traversing the sun will soon become a monsoon.

Our insecurities become most evident when things don't go the way we want them to. When this happens, anxiety kicks in and our need for control becomes more obvious. This need to control the people and things around us reflects inner insecurity; love trusts and flows, whereas fear controls and resists. When you feel the need to control, go deeper, and beneath the thoughts of worry you will find something greater.

When you experience inner transformation and become love-conscious, unconditional love of self becomes a force that overflows from within you in abundance. Everything flows toward you and then out toward everyone else. Love-consciousness becomes a magnetic, powerful force that attracts everything to you, and your creations exceed your expectations. You see that in reality nothing was ever missing, that everything is here and now, because when you feel complete within yourself, everything comes to you. When you are anchored in that space, you become love.

Choose love and it will come to you. Instead of focusing on what is missing, focus on giving — giving without limit.

We have been trained to think that everything is limited, and this thought brings us anxiety and insecurity, but now focus on love, and experience the unlimited abundance of creation. I invite you to create this experience within yourself, to discover the profound, permanent fulfillment that lies within your heart.

Try this:
Anchor Yourself to Banish Insecurity

Insecurity is fed by the fears of the mind and the attachment to image — *what will people think?* In order to free yourself from insecurity, when you begin to feel it, anchor yourself in something more profound. You can do this by thinking the first facet, *Praise love for this moment in its perfection*, bringing your attention into your heart (see Appendix 1, page 205, for more information). This will bring you back into conscious awareness of the present moment. Use this facet repeatedly until it brings you back into your internal space of peace, and allow the fear and insecurity to dissolve.

Loneliness

Have you ever felt a loneliness that nothing seemed to soothe? Maybe you attributed it to a lack of support from your loved ones or to the absence of a partner, a friend, or a family member.

Maybe you were far from home, having trouble settling in or feeling as though you didn't belong in your new neighborhood. Maybe you felt as if you had left your heart behind, in the hands of your beloved.

Whatever the cause, the feeling of loneliness stifles the heart and chokes the throat, leaving us introverted, panicked, and anxious. Often we have this feeling even when surrounded by people — emotional scars, self-defense mechanisms, and other protections make us impermeable to the affection of others. Even the celebrated American actress and sex symbol Marilyn Monroe, a woman who could surely never have lacked companionship, suffered this feeling of solitude: "I am alone — I am always alone, no matter what," she wrote in her diary (published in Marilyn Monroe, *Fragments: Poems, Intimate Notes, Letters*).

In this state of inner discontent, we cannot receive. We cannot perceive the gifts life offers, because we have closed the doors on joy and contentment. Maybe we cling to the past, perceiving our happiness as confined to some earlier time — a past relationship, a past job, when we lived in a different country, when we had different friends, when we had a different financial situation, when we had our youth or our health...

I invite you to discover the comfort and companionship that are waiting to be awakened deep within you, here and now. When we expand unconditional love within us, freeing ourselves from the fears and emotional baggage that exhaust and separate us, loneliness can no longer exist.

Love-consciousness is never lonely. You know this if you have ever observed a child playing alone, engrossed in his own imagination, feeling complete within himself. He creates his own entertainment, within the joy that arises in his being.

TRY THIS: APPRECIATE EVERYTHING

Whenever you feel lonely, as though something is missing, instead of looking outward in a search that inevitably leaves you empty-handed, focus on appreciating even the smallest things that surround you. Start with the tiniest flower you almost stepped on without noticing — appreciate that within its smallness it expresses the most perfect lines and forms and the most delicate, sweet aroma. Appreciate the child playing, the dog guarding its bone, the mother carrying her baby, the couple walking arm in arm, enveloped in each other as if nothing else existed, the cloud reaching out to cover the sun, even the chaotic symphony of the traffic. What will happen if you look at everything through the eyes of appreciation? You will notice that something in your chest begins to open, and suddenly you will surprise yourself with a smile that bubbles up from within.

To appreciate is to say yes to everything. Soon you will find that your very being emanates that *yes*, attracting the attention of others who also vibrate on that wavelength. However, it is important that you make this change without expectations — not in order to get something but just to experience this moment from a new perspective.

Start appreciating today. Then listen to yourself, deep inside: you will find that loneliness is nowhere to be found.

CHAPTER SIXTEEN

Embodying Peace
The Antidote to Living in a World of Uncertainty

Today, more than ever before, humanity is facing uncertainty. In the midst of global economic crisis and fears of climate change, our vision for the future is blurred. Humanity is restless: how can we find security in an uncertain world?

In Western society, we have learned to look for security in the wrong place: we look for it outside of ourselves. The people and things that surround us will always fail to reassure us; the nagging fear that everything could change in an instant will always be present, until, inevitably, things do change. Solid marriages are torn apart by infidelity, twenty-year careers are cut short by an unexpected change in company policy, and a lifetime's worth of savings evaporate in an instant at the hands of a corrupt investor. The outside world has never held promises for safety, a reality that we often prefer to ignore.

As humans, we tend to focus on our differences. The things that set us apart from those around us, that make us feel superior or inferior, are what stand out, yet the truly important things in life are universal, and the same in each of us. The most fundamental and powerful thing we all share is our capacity for love.

The nature of love is a mystery, not because it is impossible to discover, but because it is impossible to explain. Love reaches beyond the scope of the intellect, just as no cup can ever hold the depths of the ocean. Yet experiencing love not only is possible but is the most natural thing in the world. I'm not talking about the love we feel for another; I'm talking about the presence of love in everything, the energy that is our very being. It manifests itself as the proverbial religious experience, the peace that passes understanding, nirvana. It is the only thing that can fill the human heart. It's what I call love-consciousness.

In a world of increasing uncertainty, every one of us has the responsibility to make a difference by becoming love-consciousness and emanating peace. We can wage war upon nations, but that is not going to change things. Terrorism cannot be stopped by war, just as a fire cannot be put out with more fire. Yet although this may be true, it is useless to blame the politicians, or even war itself. If we cannot find inner peace, how can we expect to create a world that is peaceful and harmonious? Our own minds, full of dissonant chatter and confusion, are the source of our insecurity. Our actions arise from our thoughts, from our feelings. If we are full of fear, how can we contribute to creating a loving world family?

When Bill Clinton asked Nelson Mandela if he felt hatred toward his oppressors, Mandela replied, "I realized that if I kept hating them once I got in that car and got through the gate, I would still be in prison. So, I let it go, because I wanted to be free."

In the quest for peace, there is something very concrete that we can all do to contribute. In every moment, we can make a choice, the choice to rest in the abiding peace that lies within us right now and that nobody can take away from us. Instead of depending on our surroundings, which has only filled us with fear, we can learn to depend on our inner state and find a security that is always pristine and untouched, that no terrorist attack can cast a shadow on or threat of destruction shake.

The heavens have given us humans free will: the power of choice. As a consequence, it is impossible to predict the outcome of humanity, for our reality is redefined in every moment.

Let's fill our personal lives with peace, honesty, and transparency; that will go much farther toward contributing to world peace than any war protest.

In our society, we generally respond to change by sticking our heads in the sand. We try to pretend that it doesn't exist. We become rigid, seeking the illusory permanence of routine to make us feel safe, to feel in control. Many of us spend our lives creating the illusion of a stable environment: a dependable career, a solid marriage, financial security. Yet although striving to achieve material gain and trustworthy relationships is a wonderful thing, if we place our sense of security in these things, we are setting ourselves up for a fall, building our house on a fragile foundation. However much we try to ignore it, we are not in control of this erratic world, and we never will be. In order to find true stability, we must first come to terms with the unstable nature of the things we rely on. When we become aware of the impossibility of external permanence, we can begin to cultivate the only thing that can give true security: inner peace.

There was once a king who announced a great competition: to paint the perfect picture of peace. The winner would be awarded a prestigious title as well as land and unimaginable riches. Everyone in the kingdom started to paint — even people who had never painted before — in the hope of winning the prize. After many months of consideration, the king brought the selection down to two paintings, which were displayed in the palace for all to see.

The first painting was of a pristine lake, stretching serenely across the canvas, its expansive surface reflecting the snow-capped mountains behind with perfect clarity. All those who gazed upon the painting gasped in awe; surely it had to be the winner.

The second painting was quite confusing. It depicted a similar lake in the throes of a great storm, wind thrashing through the trees, the lake's surface a choppy, swirling chaos. Where was the peace in this painting? Everyone agreed, the first painting was perfect — how could this one possibly compete against it? "Look a little more closely," said the king, in response to these queries. "At the end of the branch of that tree there is a bird. He is sitting, perfectly still, in absolute peace."

That bird represents true serenity; when we can find calm within the storm of life, then we have found perfect peace.

Let's embrace the changes in our world from a place of positivity. We are moving into a new precedent, a world with elevating values and hopes. If we cling to what has come before, we will suffer. The old must die to make way for the new. Birth and death are the nature of evolution.

The world is delightfully unpredictable — just when we think we have everything nicely boxed and categorized, Michelle Obama goes and hugs the queen. Rules are made to be broken, and the laws we often live our lives by can unravel in an instant, in the right circumstances. In our quest for self-discovery, we must be willing to question our ideas and convictions, and challenge our own opinions about the world around us and, indeed, life itself. If we can remain flexible and adaptable in the face of change, we can embrace the new opportunities of a world that none of us can envision in its entirety.

Crisis is what you make of it. You can see it as a threat to your security, or you can use it as a tool to find inner stability. Sometimes our greatest losses can become our greatest opportunities; whether you wallow in the ashes or rise up transformed depends on whether you make use of the situation to grow.

THE EVOLUTION OF CONSCIOUSNESS

In the beginning, we look for answers. We dwell in the illusory. We do what society says we should do, or, conversely, we rebel and do the opposite. We create families and build businesses, yet no matter what we achieve externally, we still feel there is something missing. For some, this sense of lack comes as a deafening shout; for others, as a niggling unrest at the back of their minds; but the feeling is the same: *there must be more, there must be more*. The heart yearns for something greater.

At first we try to change the external. Some try physical transformation, others seek change in the realm of politics, through society, or within the family; we are constantly trying to reform the outside. When something makes us uncomfortable — whether it's the beggar on the street, the annoying neighbor, or an ex-lover — we try to turn a blind eye to it or remove it from our lives... but it keeps coming back, again and again, so again we try to change it. If we have an argument or we dislike something, what do we do? We separate ourselves from that person or thing. We keep separating and separating until at some point we realize that we keep repeating the same patterns. The reason is that everything external is an aspect of ourselves. Finally we realize we have to take a different approach.

There is no separation.
I am the ceiling, the floor,
the wall, the door.
There is nothing I am not.

Imagine you are a projector shining your light onto a blank wall. Then imagine that a slide is put into your slot, with an image of violent conflict. In dismay, you turn away to avoid the image, yet the same image continues to appear on the new surface you now face. You break down the wall, and the image continues to project onto the wall behind. You run away, yet you carry the image with you, and it is reflected back wherever you go. Such is the futility of our attempts to change the world: we will never be satisfied until we go inward and change our slide.

As I mentioned previously, at the age of twenty-eight I lost everything. At the time I thought it was the worst year of my life, but in reality it was the best. It was the greatest gift I could have received, because it brought me to find myself. I had to find something more secure, and that something was unconditional love. That's who we are; it lies within us. When we start to heal, we find this place. It's not just a peaceful, sweet place where we feel joy; it's also the place that has all the answers. It knows the truth, it speaks from omniscience, and when you start to connect with this place, this space of unity, you discover yourself, your true essence. This is what the heart aches for.

Today, life is moving at an ever-increasing pace. As our capacities to communicate and to consume accelerate, so does the collective seeking of humanity. The onslaught of entertainment, advertising, and distraction is coming so fast and so furious that ultimately we have to give up our attempts to find comfort there. We have to go in and find what we are really looking for: the experience of love-consciousness, the unlimited energy that connects us with totality. We have to start becoming creators and take total responsibility for our lives instead of constantly blaming the external. The way we do that is to heal and come back to our true nature, which is emptiness, vibrating in love. Abundance vibrating in love.

Future transformation is not important. What is important is what we're choosing in this moment. Ask yourself these questions: *Am I choosing love? Am I choosing to be responsible? Am I choosing to change my life? Am I putting unconditional love above everything and trusting in that? When I see external insecurity, am I being internal security? Am I evolving, or am I isolating myself in more fear?*

By going inward you can start to find the answers, your answers. Not my answers — they are not important. This is not a philosophy or a belief system; it's about you finding the guru within you, and that takes responsibility. We always want someone else to fix us, but they can't. You can't just take yourself to the mechanic to get fixed as you can with your car.

No one can fix you...you have to fix your self.

You have to go into your depths, but this is the wonder of the exploration of self: it's the most exciting thing — the only land that remains undiscovered. When you start to discover yourself you will be amazed with how incredible you are, how brave you've been, and the choices you have made.

There once was a powerful magician who was visited by a mouse. "Oh, great wizard," squeaked the mouse, "I am terrified of cats! They chase me everywhere. I can't get a moment's peace! Please help." In a puff of smoke, the magician transformed the mouse into a cat. A week later, the cat returned. "Oh, great wizard, I'm at my wit's end! The cats are bothering me no longer — and for that I am very grateful — but have you any idea how many dogs there are in this neighborhood?!" With a puff of smoke, the magician turned him into a dog. A week later, the dog returned. *"Great wizard, the dogs are no longer causing me any trouble, but I have heard the most awful stories about tigers coming into the village. Their favorite food is us dogs!" With a tired smile, the magician turned him into a tiger. A week later, the tiger came back to the magician. "Oh, great wizard, you have no idea how many hunters there are in the jungle —"*

Before he could finish, the wizard replied, "It doesn't matter what I turn you into, you still have the heart of a mouse."

We can change our external circumstances as much as we like, but until we go inward and heal the root of our insecurity, we will always be a victim of fear.

Peace without Prerequisites

Peace — a word that unites humanity in its common desire for union. Even those who fight are fighting for peace. Most of us think of peace in the following way: *There is something wrong with the world. We must reach a state (of peace) in order to make things right.*

Have you noticed that when people are asking for peace, they're usually screaming?

I want to be in peace!

Leave me in peace!

Turn off that noise! I want some peace!!!

As humans, we are always saying, "I want to be in peace," but then the next minute we're fighting for "justice," fighting to be right. So what's really more important — finding peace or being right? When we become attached to our point of view, it can become more important to us than anything else. This need to be right, which often requires proving the other wrong, generates conflict.

Where are you fighting in your life? Where has your opinion become more important than peace, than harmony?

If you are dissatisfied with the world and wishing for a more peaceful human family, your dissatisfaction is not contributing to peace in this moment.

Peace is stillness in the midst of rush-hour traffic.

Peace is inner acceptance.

Peace is surrender: surrender to what is, relinquishing the fight and the need to prove a point.

Peace is the innocent joy of being,

The joy of existence,

The awareness of perfection.

Yes, we hope for a world free from conflict, but waiting around for the world to change doesn't help matters. Change yourself, and then you will be contributing in the most profound and effective way to the creation of a peaceful planet.

This is the time and the place. They are the only time and place that exist, for both time and space are illusion. In the unity of love-consciousness, there is no distance, there is nothing happening, no change to measure. There only is. Everything else is a lie. When you are present with yourself, you are at peace. You are one with what is; you reconcile your misgivings with life and embrace your reality. This is power, this is life. Anything else is merely distraction. You can change your energy in an instant by being fully present with yourself.

Sure, you might have heard all this before, but you haven't heard it enough until it becomes your reality. You haven't heard it enough until you commit your every moment to being present, to reuniting with your true self. I found the way to do it. It worked for me. It works for many. It can work for you.

STAYING THE COURSE

When we start to expand our consciousness, its voice begins to overshadow the vacillations of the intellect. The mind can perceive only within the constraints of duality, so when we start to live from union, the mind becomes secondary; once the voice of the heart takes charge, the mind no longer has the upper hand. This terrifies the mind, which feels its control slipping away, and so it tries to quash the voice of love-consciousness.

What happens when the mind yields its control? You start to be present, anchored within self, trusting what comes while sitting in a place of peace and joy. Then the mind becomes your servant, instead of your being a servant to its dualities and doubts. This frightens the intellect, and as you get closer to that point it becomes frantic. In its last desperate bid for dominance, it will try everything it can to manipulate you and keep you in a place of fear.

If you're not feeling joy, it's not love-consciousness.

In those moments, just remember, *If you're not feeling joy, it's not love-consciousness.* It's easy to tell the difference: if you feel confusion, fear, craving, or uncertainty, you're stuck in the intellect. Once you notice those feelings, stop and ask yourself what you want to focus on, fear or love? The answer to this question is very simple, and it's always the same: always choose the love.

The facets of the Isha System are the perfect way to train the mind to automatically choose the plenitude of love-consciousness (see Appendix 1, page 205).

The Simplicity of True Spirituality

The so-called spiritual world is rife with distractions in the form of trappings, traditions, and customs. As a result, spirituality often seems complex and confusing, when in reality it is quite the opposite. From astrological analysis to the study of different realms to worrying about what color clothing we are wearing, which way our house is facing, how our hair is cut, or traveling to "sacred ground," we place more importance on external conditions than on what we are experiencing internally. By the time we have finished checking to see that all our conditions are in place, we have already lost the opportunities the day brings to find the joy and beauty of life. Simplicity is the hallmark of authentic spirituality, for life is simple, love is simple, and complexity does nothing more than feed the intellect.

It amazes me how much importance we attach to tradition. We think that because generations before us always did something a certain way, that behavior is somehow more valuable, more sacred, more righteous. Yet we only have to look at our personal lives to see that repetitive behaviors are not necessarily beneficial. Would we extoll the benefits of smoking cigarettes just because we had done it for many years? It's traditional! This blind following of tradition is particularly fascinating to me when it comes to spirituality.

Many of us choose our beliefs based on what generations before us have done. Yet spirituality is about growth; it is about evolution. It is about letting go of that which has come before and embracing a new perception of reality. Moreover, it is about discovering the truth within ourselves, not adhering to the status quo. Maybe this is why so few have reached realization — because even in our search for meaning we prefer to follow the herd; even when the heart begins to question that which we are accustomed to, we are easily drawn onto another well-trodden road. I think that tradition makes us feel safe; it lends authority and weight to our convictions. But convictions are a poor substitute for experience. When you have a spiritual experience of your own, you will feel little need to convince others of your perspective or demonstrate the validity of your inner discovery.

When exploring spirituality, don't look for that which makes you feel comfortable or safe. Look outside the box; head toward uncertainty. Only by going beyond that which is already known can we make the true discovery.

THE END OF SEEKING

Some years ago, I was being interviewed by the editor of a spiritual magazine. She was clearly a very spiritual person who had dedicated many years of her life to her search, and we were both enjoying the interview very much.

Suddenly a strange thing happened. She asked me what I

was searching for. I replied that my search had ended, that I had found what I was seeking.

She was shocked! She couldn't accept the idea that the search could end. She was so offended that she finished the interview almost immediately, and it was never published. At first I couldn't understand what had happened for such a positive interview to change so abruptly. Afterward, I realized: she was addicted to searching. The idea of ending her search, of actually finding what she was looking for, frightened her, because she had identified so much with the role of seeker. She thought it was who she was. If she stopped seeking, "she" would cease to exist.

This is actually true for all of us: what we are most afraid of is the stillness of love-consciousness. We can't comprehend what it would mean to stop the search, when in reality it would simply mean being in this moment, ad infinitum. But most of us have already learned that we cannot stay present for more than a few instants. We keep distracting ourselves with the workings of our minds, lest we might face the truth.

What I am proposing is an end to the search. The search keeps us looking outward, off into the horizon of an imaginary ideal future. This searching will never end — until we take our eyes away from the distance and focus them on the now. When we do so, we awaken, and that awakening is the end; it is the end of suffering, the end of running, the end of hiding. It is a kind of death: the death of the illusory self, the death of fear. It is about eliminating, burning away that which does not serve, and from the ashes rising free in the unlimited expanses of pure being; in ever-present, omniscient awareness, all embracing, all accepting.

Now that I have found completion, what is there left to do? Only to give. This is how teachers sprout from awakening. True teachers do not seek to teach; they seek to self-realize. Then, from their realization, teaching flows spontaneously, like water from a spring. There is no effort there, for it is the nature of love to share, the only desire of the heart to serve other hearts in their awakening.

The end is the beginning, and now that I am empty, I am finally full.

With love,
Isha

The Isha System

The Isha System is revolutionizing spirituality throughout the world. Its teachings are practical and easy to incorporate into daily life, yet they produce a profound inner transformation, returning us to a place of self-love and unlocking the door to enlightenment.

Explained in its entirety in the book and movie *Why Walk When You Can Fly?* the system can be easily learned and practiced by all, regardless of age, creed, or conditioning.

One of the cornerstones of the Isha System is the practice of the Isha facets. These four facets are brief statements of eternal truths that we repeat to ourselves, ideally for an hour a day, every day, with our eyes closed. Many people notice uplifting, transformational effects immediately; for others the benefits emerge after a few days or weeks of practice. The facets are as follows:

Praise love for this moment in its perfection.

As you think this facet, place your attention deep in your heart.

Thank love for my human experience in its perfection.

As you think this facet, place your attention deep in your heart.

Love creates me in my perfection.

As you think this facet, place your attention deep in your heart.

Om unity.

As you think this facet, bring your attention from the base of your spine to the top of your head.

It is important not to change the facets: the wording is very specific, and the facets are most effective when done as stated. The facets are designed to take us beyond the intellect, so the intellect's opinion of how the facets could be changed or "improved" is not the best guide!

How to Practice

Sit comfortably or lie down, and close your eyes. Gently think the facet, placing your attention as indicated, and then wait a few seconds, allowing thoughts to come and go naturally. Don't try to avoid thoughts or silence the mind; just embrace whatever comes. Then again think the facet, placing your attention as indicated, and again wait a few moments. Sometimes the gap between repetitions will be quite short, sometimes quite long. Sometimes you will forget to think the facet and wander off. When you realize this has happened, simply think the facet again. You never need to control or strain: the practice of the facets should always be gentle and natural.

TIMING

You can divide your hour of daily practice into two half-hour sessions or three of twenty minutes. In each session, use the facets in order for equal amounts of time. For example, a twenty-minute session should begin with five minutes of the first facet and then move on to five of the second, five of the third, and finally five minutes of the fourth. You can check the time by glancing at your watch, and it doesn't have to be exact! Remember, the practice should be gentle, so don't worry about rigidly adhering to the time frame. If you fall asleep, that's fine; you might try sitting instead of lying down if you find you can never stay awake.

The most effective way to integrate the facets into your awareness and gain a deeper understanding of the Isha System as a whole is to participate in an Isha System seminar. Visit www.ishajudd.com to find extensive information about upcoming events and support groups around the world.

APPENDIX TWO

"La I" Uruguay and "La I" Mexico
Spas for Consciousness

*I*sha has founded two beautiful centers for the expansion of love-consciousness, "La I" Uruguay and "La I" Mexico. A visit to either of these centers is an opportunity to dive within and deepen your experience of love-consciousness. During your stay, we will provide you with everything you need to take full advantage of your process of growth, including round-the-clock support from teachers personally trained by Isha.

Isha's "La I" centers offer a new concept in vacations. A visit to "La I" is not about escaping from life or "getting away from it all" — it is about returning to your heart. A vacation at "La I" is a journey back inward. It is the ultimate adventure — into your being, your essence. We invite you to come and explore your inner depths, to have the perfect holiday romance with the best companion you could ever find...yourself.

Love Has Wings

For more information and for reservations, contact us:

In the United States: (305) 390 2709
In Mexico: (+52) 314 3341414
In Uruguay: (+598) 437 36994
reservations@ishajudd.com
www.ishajudd.com

ABOUT THE AUTHOR

*O*riginally from Australia, Isha has lived since 2000 in South America, where she has built a large following as a writer and teacher. She is the founder of Isha Educating for Peace, a self-funded NGO that provides thousands throughout the continent with free access to her teachings. Working with children, politicians, prisoners, and people with disabilities, the organization aims to support the underprivileged in all areas of society. In 2010, Isha taught over six thousand people affected by the earthquakes in the south of Chile in a special event. She was recently named Ambassador for Peace by the Argentinean Senate, and Citizen of the World by the International University of Cuernavaca, Mexico. She lives in Uruguay with the teachers she has trained in her system, as well as a multitude of animals.

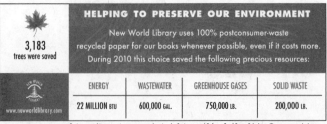

HELPING TO PRESERVE OUR ENVIRONMENT

3,183
trees were saved

New World Library uses 100% postconsumer-waste recycled paper for our books whenever possible, even if it costs more. During 2010 this choice saved the following precious resources:

	ENERGY	WASTEWATER	GREENHOUSE GASES	SOLID WASTE
www.newworldlibrary.com	22 MILLION BTU	600,000 GAL.	750,000 LB.	200,000 LB.

Environmental impact estimates were made using the Environmental Defense Fund Paper Calculator @ www.papercalculator.org.